Discovery Learning in the Primary School

Discovery Learning in the Primary School

John Foster

Deputy Principal,
Lady Mabel College of Education, Wentworth, Rotherham

LONDON AND BOSTON
ROUTLEDGE & KEGAN PAUL

First published 1972
by Routledge & Kegan Paul Ltd
Broadway House, 68-74 Carter Lane,
London EC4V 5EL and
9 Park Street,
Boston, Mass. 02108, U.S.A.

Printed in Great Britain by
Northumberland Press Ltd
Gateshead

ISBN 0 7100 7356 9 (c)
ISBN 0 7100 7357 7 (p)

THE STUDENTS LIBRARY OF EDUCATION has been designed to meet the needs of students of Education at Colleges of Education and at University Institutes and Departments. It will also be valuable for practising teachers and education- ists. The series takes full account of the latest developments in teacher-training and of new methods and approaches in education. Separate volumes will provide authoritative and up-to-date accounts of the topics within the major fields of sociology, philosophy and history of education, educational psychology, and method. Care has been taken that special- ist topics are treated lucidly and usefully for the non- specialist reader. Altogether, the Students Library of Education will provide a comprehensive introduction and guide to anyone concerned with the study of education, and with educational theory and practice.

Contents

Acknowledgments

I would like to thank all the teachers, students, and children whose help made this book possible. My thanks are especially due to the staff and children of Haughton Green County Primary School during the period when I was headmaster there. Students and staff at Manchester College of Education have assisted me enormously. Teachers attending Froebel Courses, with whom I worked, provided me me with a wealth of excellent material for which I am grateful.

1

Introduction

The aim of the book

The aim of this book is to describe and analyse a number of informal learning situations, to examine some of the educational principles involved, and to assess the success of the methods and techniques used. Both teachers and students have collected the material from many sources. Some of it is quite original but other ideas are typical of much of the work found in primary schools today.

All the work described has arisen from working along active lines with children. For the most part, conditions have not been ideal. The school where I was headmaster was a building first occupied in 1904. It was suitable for about 200 children, but at one time, there were 385 on the roll. Other work went on in similar situations and I cannot recall any work quoted which was carried out under ideal conditions. Overcrowding, teacher shortage, and lack of basic supplies were taken for granted, but in every school there were enterprising, resourceful, and energetic teachers who were deeply concerned about the quality of the education with which they were associated.

In some cases, where there were students to help in the classroom, pupil/teacher ratios were low. In others, the ratio was one teacher to forty-nine children.

I have tried to write this account simply, in non-technical terms. The book is descriptive but, I hope, it is also objective. Work described has been compared to similar studies and evaluated in the light of other findings. I hope, therefore, that the book will be some help to teachers in the constant re-appraisal of their own ideas and teaching methods.

Teaching by informal methods is not confined to young teachers or indeed to teachers who profess to be 'progressive'. Some of the best discovery learning I have seen has been in the classrooms of teachers who would have rated themselves 'formalists'. In fact, they were formal in a very limited sphere but they were wholly aware of the children in their classes and always prepared to adapt their ideas to the changing needs of their pupils.

Teachers and students must ask themselves some basic questions. The complete answers to these questions will seldom be found in textbooks of education, but these books will contain ideas which can be sifted and tested in the classroom. It is the 'thinking' teacher who can take both first- and second-hand experiences and resolve, blend, re-create, and make them his own, who will be the steadiest guide for discovery learning. Teachers must decide for themselves how much they should change, the direction of the changes, and the speed with which they are carried out. What is right for one will be quite impossible for another. There is no right or wrong way but an appropriate approach for each person in each encounter.

My own feeling about discovery learning is that it must be firmly based on order, with a flexible basic organization

2

that the children can understand and within which they can work freely. In the classroom, materials should be readily available and yet tidily stored, children should be conscious of tidiness but not inhibited by it. They should be free to gather and use the materials they require but at the same time they need to be aware of the need for economy. These principles can be applied even in classrooms where physical conditions are bad, although it is not easy in these circumstances. In surroundings like this, the need is for an inventive, planning teacher with a creative turn of mind, one with a flair for the unusual and the ability to convert. I believe that educational suppliers would do well to examine carefully some of the conversions of furniture that teachers work out. These surely should be a basis for the kind of equipment teachers really require.

This book analyses the learning of children individually and in small groups, as members of a class, and of the whole school. All these arrangements have their influence on children's learning and there is constant fluidity in the groupings. Children move easily from one group to another as the emphasis of their work and interest changes. Basically, I have looked closely to see the effect of the primary school of today on the total well-being of the child, not only in school but at home and in the community.

As well as examining the practical side of discovery, I have discussed here the theory of discovery methods and attempted to show why they were used and what principles have guided their development. So that teachers may begin to understand the present position more fully, I have included a brief outline of the development of this approach so that the work in schools today can be seen as part of an ever-developing pattern.

The rather long bibliography is a comprehensive selection from more important writings about theory and practice in the modern primary school. I have referred directly in the text to many of these books, and less directly to the authors of others; some of the books I have not mentioned at all. The bibliography is there so that teachers may follow up any aspect of the work that particularly interests them in books that deal more specifically with the various themes and ideas in this book. It is as well to notice the date of publication of the books listed. Sometimes, these are not recent, but they are included as they often represent most accurately the thinking current at that period. These books must be viewed in their own context and not always be taken as typical of practice today.

The nature of discovery learning

The natural activities of a young child are nearly all learning situations involving interactions with the environment. I remember one morning awakening Suzanne, aged nine years. One moment she was in a deep sleep—the next moment, without any conscious effort, she launched into a spate of questions, thoughts, comments, hopes, inquiries, and speculation about the day's activities. This wakening moment set the pattern of the natural activity of the day for her. It typifies the approach of lively, healthy, primary school children to life generally, and consequently to learning. Underlying most of the activities of a young child is a tireless curiosity, and a desire to find out through personal exploration. In this way, a child is helped to form new concepts of increasing complexity and is able to enlarge and revise the ideas he has met before. All the time, he is taking in information and using it to help to clarify and refine what he already knows. He brings much from past experience to every learning situation and he needs to be constantly challenged so that he can test the accuracy and validity of his accumulated experiences. By a kind of scanning process he is able to select information relevant to the problem on hand, and by degrees to formulate ideas about the possibility of the results of any subsequent action he may take. He is framing a simple hypothesis which he can then test by personal experiment. This is a continuing process which is developing and refining his ideas the whole time. He is learning to anticipate the results of his actions and formulate ideas of cause and effect. 'If I take this brick away, then the building will fall.' The two operative ideas he is learning to handle are, 'If ... then ...'. It is this kind of thinking, at best spontaneous, based on the following up and extension of natural interests, which is the discovery learning evaluated in this book.

The use of the word 'discovery' in schools is comparatively recent. It has come to be used as an omnibus term sometimes covering the full range of good primary school work. I prefer to use it as it is used in the Plowden (1967) report where learning by discovery is seen as stemming from 'initial curiosity, often stimulated by the environment the teacher provides, leading to questions and to a consideration of what questions it is sensible to ask and how to find the answers ... essential elements are enquiry, exploration and first hand experience'.

Implicit in this concept of discovery learning is the whole question of the relationship between the teacher and the child. Active learning does not flourish in the authoritarian classroom. The role of the teacher in the discovery classroom becomes more advisory than formally and openly didactic, more one of guidance than dispenser of factual information. The nature of discovery as exemplified in this book can be seen as a fundamental aspect of most vivid learning experiences of young children. Where the experience has been intense, where there has been a lively stimulation and imaginative encouragement by the teacher, where there has been creative problem-solving, and the exercise of choice before considered judgments have been made, the principles of discovery learning have been realized.

In reviewing American literature regarding learning by discovery, Kersch and Wittrock (1967) describe discovery learning as that completed with little or no help from the teacher. I believe that discovery learning of this type has little place in English primary education at this time. It suggests an abdication by the teacher of his responsibility of arranging children's learning in an ordered, often sequential manner. It is when teachers misunderstand discovery learning approaches, and assume that a policy of 'non-intervention' into children's learning is the order of the day, that failures occur. First and foremost, a teacher must be concerned with quality. He must be constantly aware of the need to ensure progression, and check that some measure of improvement is taking place. This will only happen if he guides the discovery, and ensures that he knows exactly what each child in the class is doing at a particular time, and has some machinery for ascertaining how well he is doing it. The sequence is usually as follows: first, aims and objectives of the particular activity are thought out and documented. Then, learning experiences are devised which rely on a form of guided discovery, so that the final act of finding-out belongs to the child. These activities should be specifically designed to try to achieve the stated aims and objectives. Finally, some evaluation needs to be carried out to assess to what degree the aims and objectives have been reached. In this way, the objectives of the next activities are indicated, and the process becomes an organized pattern.

In the research field, many attempts have been made to compare the effectiveness of pure discovery, guided discovery, and pure reception, but little conclusive evidence is available as to the relative value of these systems. Interested readers may wish to consult Shulman and Keislar (1966), Bassett (1970), and Rowell, Simon and Wiseman (1969) for the details of this research. In my context, it appears that teachers are best advised to take the pragmatic view advocated by Bruner (1961) to 'develop the best pedagogy you can'. This implies using a mixture of psychology, common sense and professional intuition to develop a system based on clinical observation of children's activities, and cautious changes of methods and techniques at the point when success in a particular activity looks obtainable. As a general principle, the more informal the learning arrangements become in a school, the greater is the need for a teacher to prepare a system which permits individual and group inquiry, with frequent teacher contact, and for him also to plan a method of noting the content and degree of success achieved by individual children. Detailed suggestions of some of the ways this can be done, and the role of the teacher in carrying out this idea, will be found throughout the book as different learning situations are described and analysed.

In school, discovery learning will often involve a contrived experience, usually in the form of a stimulus from the teacher, the focal point of which has arisen out of an interest of the children. The skilful teacher arranges for the extension of this shared experience so that each child concerned can develop it in the most effective way for him personally. In fact, the success of the stimulus can often be judged by the variety of responses it elicits in a group of children. A teacher in a classroom I visited recently showed me a collection of book matches brought in by a boy whose father was an airline steward. These matches had been gathered from all over the world and were well displayed on a coloured background. Some of the books of matches had been arranged on a side table with reference material linking them with their country of origin. There were also some cards inviting thought and comment, and others suggesting ideas for activities which could be based on the books of matches. It was three weeks before I visited this classroom again. Work had developed on individual lines. About eight out of a class of forty-two had begun work on the theme, but all of them had chosen different aspects. One girl had studied cover designs and made a booklet reproducing these and designing others of her own. Two children had begun to study places from which the matches had come. Many of the book matches showed pictures of people in local dress. One girl had made models of the figures and had written descriptions of the costumes. One boy had written to a firm making book matches and found out how matches were made. This had led to a study of wood and paper as it is used in match making. Another boy had arranged experiments to see the relative burning time of different types of matches, while another had compared costs of matches, boxes against books, wholesale against retail prices. He had then graphed the numbers in boxes of matches produced by different firms. The last child concerned, a girl, had prepared a talk for the class on all the work arising from the display. The follow-up had been completely individual, reflecting a personal response which was most appropriate, at that time, for any one of the children. But there was no response at all from more than three-quarters of the children in this class. This is not unusual and brings out an important point. The inexperienced teacher will sometimes look for a response from every child or will become worried if a stimulus fails. It is the perceptive teacher who accepts that many ideas will be taken up only by some children. This he must accept if the work is to be geared to individual needs. The length of time each child works and his interest span will also vary considerably. Flexibility of organization, therefore, is an essential feature of the discovery learning classroom.

At a teachers' course, I was once asked about children who did not seem to respond to any stimulus of the kind discussed here. Teachers do meet this problem, and faced with a child who does not respond easily, must take a broader, more long-term view of the problem. It is rare that the emotional value-judgment, often made on the spot, will be very valid. The teacher will probably make a more realistic appraisal of the problem if he returns to it at a later point. In this dilemma, he has a strong ally in the natural curiosity of the child. All children have this urge, which shows itself as inquisitiveness and a surprising eagerness when it is aroused. However, in some cases, ingenuity is needed before this source of energy is evident. The reason for the lack of response will most likely be very complex; it will be basically emotional, and in many cases a good personal relationship between the teacher and the child will be the first essential towards arriving at the point where curiosity can be positively evoked and the child will respond. The difficult journey towards the first successful response will usually be made with an air of finding out

9

together, the child and teacher making the first tentative steps side by side so that when confidence is gained and success experienced, the teacher is able to withdraw, and the child is usually eager to go on.

Good discovery learning will usually be accompanied by the children's recording of their findings. The teacher can use this to link the acquisition of skills with creative activities. In this way, there is motivation for children to learn skills which appear to be a necessary adjunct to their most enjoyable activities. It is, therefore, necessary that they should be given opportunities for a variety of experiences which can be symbolized in as many ways as possible. The teacher has an important role to play in devising tasks that will have a compelling impact on the children. If these contrived situations lead to great interest, they will be a spur to the learning of skills through which experiences can be re-created—speech, writing, painting, modelling, movement or any other form of expression.

In primary education today, there is a strong emphasis on the full, all-round development of the child. Rote learning has long been discredited. Indeed, even the learning of an agreed content of information has now receded since there have been widespread challenges of the relevance to present-day living of much that used to be considered traditional in the curriculum. Competence in reading and arithmetic, once the aim of elementary education, are now merely two components of many requirements which children need in order to equip themselves for their roles as adults. Teachers have then to ask fundamental questions about the objectives of primary education. Since it is no longer possible to lay down a set of facts which should be known or even to define probable areas of interest which children will follow, one of the fundamental purposes in primary schools should be to help children to think for themselves, to exercise choice, to make judgments, and to discriminate. The emphasis must be on the process of learning rather than on the end product. Discovery, sifting through a variety of possibilities, general inquiry, must be encouraged as being important in themselves—for what they are and not for what their end-product may be. Teachers must be concerned with the quality of children's learning; they must be aware of its progressive complexity and arrange for an individual approach which grows out of personal discovery and allows for development through widening interests. The work described in this book shows how the control of the learning sequence, in a discovery approach, passes progressively from teacher to learner. The emphasis is on a total approach which stresses all-round development, and an integrated presentation of material which is a challenge to the child. When the child takes up this challenge and is involved in both creative and logical thinking, effective discovery learning is likely. Ausubel (1963) attacks discovery approaches, maintaining that they are often uneconomical and that many concepts are better introduced, for some children, by other methods. Certainly, children do not 'discover' everything we want them to without help. It is a fallacy that the teacher should not structure the child's learning. In fact, the role of the teacher is to assist in regulating the children's experiences so that they can discover easily for themselves. In this structured approach, a child is trained to think for himself in an ordered manner. The teacher encourages him to use an imaginative attack, but at the same time makes the comments which will encourage him to submit his thinking to the test of experiment. The question, 'What will happen if you change the order?' or, 'Can you find any other ways of getting the answer?' will suggest different viewpoints and help a child to educe principles for himself.

The young child's play has often been compared to the work of the scientist. In his natural learning, often seen in nursery school play, a child can be found trying to work out the consequences of his actions. He poses simple problems and tests the possibilities for action. He classifies, categorizes, and assembles his playthings in ordered sequence. In the discovery classroom, the teacher needs to provide opportunities for this experimenting to take place. However, provision is not enough. The teacher needs the skill to know when to step in and help, and when to allow the child to adventure freely. The acquisition of this skill is helped by experience but can be aided by a full understanding of the principles of how children form concepts. A knowledge of the complexities of the thinking processes is also useful. Russell (1956) discusses the ingredients of thinking and highlights several aspects which are useful indicators of the scope of a child's cognitive activity when he is thinking about everyday problems. He shows how a child selects, by perception, from a wealth of sensations and orders them into gradually forming concepts. This activity involves searching, manipulating, and organizing, beginning with crude, undirected thought through to inductive thinking, problem solving, critical and creative thinking. The teacher can certainly help a child better if he has a good knowledge of the child's previous experiences and if he is able to identify the situations in which a child works best. For example, some children may work better as part of a team while others think better working alone. One child may be able to establish the privacy he needs in order to think amidst a host of classroom activities, while another child may require to be segregated completely.

The picture emerging from the principles discussed is that most of what we learn depends on, and is made possible by, what we know already. This previous knowledge forms a framework on to which later knowledge can be built. Children need much first-hand experience if they are to be free to adventure in their learning, to follow up interesting lines of inquiry, to become aware of unfruitful lines of approach, and to evolve an overall view of the problem. At the same time, there is need for guidance from the teacher to ensure effective, economical learning. Thus, discovery learning in school involves both freedom and structure, both aspects contributing to effective learning and leading to understanding.

The evolution of discovery methods in schools

The concept of discovery learning is by no means new. Philosophers have testified to its values and throughout man's endeavours one can see examples of cultural heritage and knowledge being transmitted through participation by the learner. The apprentice has for centuries learned his trade and practised his skill by taking an active part in the work on hand. His efforts over the years are directed to more difficult tasks as he masters easy aspects of the work. The skilled worker acts as a guide—encouraging, extending, helping, and re-directing the efforts of the learner. Every young child in the family group learns through discovering new avenues of exploration and new situations to think about. Here, other members of the family help a younger child by extending his interests, drawing his attention to the unusual, and giving him the benefit of their extra experience. Religious Orders, the guilds, and many other communities concerned with education and training, arrange for the learner to follow a path which involves finding out and learning by experience through personal activity.

Examples of discovery learning can be drawn from every age. The great educators have always advocated the principles of discovery in the learning process and suggested an active approach in education. It is, however, when we look at the growth of our school systems over the last hundred years or so that we can begin to see a developing pattern of discovery learning being applied to groups of children in schools. The work of Charlotte Mason, Rachel and Margaret MacMillan, and Maria Montessori show us that enlightened, far-seeing educationists were working on active lines with young children even in the last century. They were evolving systems where children could learn through finding out. Some of their work may appear almost naïve when set against practice today but the principles they followed and the experimental work they carried out formed the basis on which later work developed. Theirs is part of the story which has brought us to our present position. It is usually principles which have been handed down and reapplied practically to the needs of today. The principles which have survived are those which have been supported by the scientific research now being made available to teachers. A good example of this is the work and teachings of Friedrich Froebel. His practical approach, involving his apparatus and stories, has no place in our schools today. The principles which he put forward, however, are clearly relevant and indeed are the essence of the thought behind the aims of progressive schools. The emphasis is on an extremely flexible arrangement which gives the maximum importance to the individual.

We can point to the work of many pioneers who worked with children on discovery lines during the early part of this century and whose work has been built on and further developed by later generations of teachers. In the early 1920s A. S. Neill began working at Summerhill on truly radical lines. He saw the aim of education as working joyfully and finding happiness. Giving the child a great deal of freedom of choice and self-determination, he stressed activities which can surely be labelled 'discovery learning'. These activities helped the child to achieve independence and assisted him to make decisions which established him as an individual willing to think positively about his problems.

Edward O'Neill, working in Lancashire about the same time, also laid great stress on children organizing their own learning and extending lines of inquiry which interested them. Holmes (1952) describes his work well and shows the degree of involvement which children achieved using these methods.

Perhaps one of the classic pieces of work of this type was undertaken by Susan Isaacs. Her work at the Malting House School, Cambridge, in the late 1920s still provides some of the best studies we have of young children learning through discovery approaches. The close observations she made of the children showed how mature their thinking could become in a highly enriched and provocative environment. However, her work could never be considered as an invitation for the teacher to stand back and 'wait until the child is ready'. Rather she illustrates continuously the very positive role the teacher plays in 'blowing-up' children's experiences so that they become more meaningful as they are seen in new ways, and as the concepts involved are re-presented for their further consideration and assimilation at a higher level of understanding.

Throughout the years, government-sponsored reports have commented on the value of discovery learning and activity approaches.

The famous quotation from the Hadow (1931) report that the 'curriculum is to be thought of in terms of activity and experience rather than of knowledge to be acquired and facts to be stored' is an illustration of the sympathy with progressive methods shown in official reports. Following and extending the suggestions in this report, many teachers began to re-appraise their aims as primary school teachers and prepare material on adventurous, discovery-based lines. *The Nursery and Infants' Schools Report*, published in 1933, advocated the extension of natural experiences as the basis of the learning activities of young children. The principles set out by Hadow were echoed and re-affirmed again in the Spens (1939) report on secondary education eight years later. This report made a strong plea for general enrichment of school life so that each child can achieve the highest degree of individual development. This far-seeing report suggested curriculum reform which is only now beginning to take place through such active learning schemes as the Outward Bound Centres and the Duke of Edinburgh Award Scheme.

Today the use of discovery methods in primary schools is widespread. No set pattern of approach exists. Rather, schools have developed according to the teaching strengths that were available, or along lines suggested by local authorities concerned with the various curriculum development schemes of the Schools' Council and similar organizations.

Sometimes, this work has been inadequately understood or misinterpreted, with the result that severe criticism has been incurred. Dearden (1968) argues, as a philosopher, that progressive education has no clearly argued rationale and attacks much of the literature as being descriptive rather that definitive.

Gardner (1969) criticizes 'the modern craze for child-centred education' specifically in the way in which reading is taught. He suggests that in schools using modern methods, reading is acquired rather than taught and that improvement would result if more systematic approaches were adopted. This feeling is reflected in recent work by Chall (1967) and is implied in the work of Bereiter and Engelmann (1966).

Is this movement paradoxical to the main line of thought in English education or can it be reconciled with the work which has become typical of progressive primary education representing the majority of schools in this country? Discussing this work and its implications with teachers, it appears that there is a danger that it will be interpreted by some teachers as 'putting the clock back', and seen as some kind of official blessing for a return to formal approaches.

It would be a pity if this view was countenanced in any way. This questioning of approaches, aims and values is a healthy, positive, re-appraisal of the valuable work being carried on in primary schools. It is, however, only pertinent criticism of those schools working along modern lines which have misinterpreted the underlying theory behind the work they are doing. These attacks can only be levelled against schools where children are given complete freedom and where there is little adult interaction with children's activities.

Good primary education, carried on in efficient schools

working on child-centred lines, acknowledges the need for a great deal of structure both in the development of creative pursuits and in the acquisition of skills. In schools of this type, there is sound basic organization, planned routine and a built-in system of order for the learning of skills, which is welded into the overall pattern of the development and sustaining of children's interests. Identification of strategies used in problem-solving, concept-formation, and 'cracking the code' aspects of reading, are essential to the teacher working on informal lines. It is essential to teachers using modern methods to see their primary functions as observing, recording and interacting with the learning activities of the children.

It is not the imposition of a structured approach which is required in primary education but adventurous use by teachers of systems which will identify success and diagnose weaknesses, so that the teachers may better ensure the promotion and activation of the child as the principal agent in his own learning.

2

Children learning by discovery individually

The work discussed in this chapter was all carried out with a mixed, unstreamed, top junior class of ten- and eleven-year-old children. The children were used to working individually and most of their assignments started off in this way. Often, however, joint interests developed and group work began.

In four pieces of work where the starting point appeared to be connected with a particular subject I shall show how the subject interest widened. In this classroom, an atmosphere existed which was akin to the one described by Reid (1962) as one of 'freedom, where the teacher and the child are open to each other'. There was a definite 'affinity' between the teacher and the children characterized by a two-way flow of giving and receiving, of educating and being educated. The topics for discussion were: 1 My interest in graphs (Mathematical), Peter; 2 My own poetry (English), Christine; 3 Sounds—my discoveries (Scientific), John; 4 Wheels (Historical), David.

My interest in graphs—Peter

During a very cold spell the teacher had asked Peter to graph the classroom temperature daily. A very thorough boy of above average intelligence, Peter had done this with diligence and considerable precision, proudly adding to his graph each day. Having finished his assignment, he asked if he could 'do some research on graphs'. Armed with some graph paper, textbooks, and a challenge card made by the teacher as a starting point and full of 'open-ended' situations requiring thought and creative problem-solving, Peter began his work.

Challenge cards were used considerably in this class, but always the aim was interpretation, problem-solving, and generalization or applying given facts to a new situation. Rowe (1959) says 'One mark of the educated man is his power to apply a few general principles to a variety of concrete particulars.... We aim to develop this power by shaping the job cards ... to ask for something more than the synthesis.' This seems to sum up our own attitudes to the challenge cards issued to these children. The point is developed under the heading *Assignment cards* at the end of this chapter.

Peter continued to chart the temperature in the classroom as a block graph, and made a line graph of the outside temperature at the same time. In his book, he noted the similarity of pattern between these two and continued by showing each as block and line for easier comparison. He also made block and line graphs to record how much milk was drunk in class each day; how many children were late each day; attendances for the week; weight of children in the class (Peter was very conscious of this, being overweight himself); popularity of pop groups; and his friends' pocket money.

Looking at the block graph one day he glanced across at some Cuisinaire rods and said, 'Hey Tony, lend me some of those blocks—I can make a model of this graph by using them.' This he soon did and proceeded to show the children who were interested the comparison in shape and how he had done this.

When the teacher suggested that he might try a circular graph he did not understand this concept. The teacher asked him to divide up the children in school into groups by age. He did this quickly using the Admission Register. The teacher began to show him how to get this information into a pie graph but Peter stopped him as soon as he realized what was required and went on to complete it unaided. He repeated this using children's birthdays.

An isotype graph from a national newspaper was new to him. He soon read it and interpreted it—I left him then and he produced a similar type of graph using pin men, each one representing ten children. (The pin men had ten strokes to complete them, his idea, and to represent six children at the end he drew only six of the ten strokes.) This drawing of men took him on to a self-portrait which led to the topic, 'Talking about me'—referred to briefly later —a topic involving art, creative writing, literature, and geography.

My own poetry—Christine

Christine was a sensitive, intelligent girl with a very retiring disposition. She became more forthcoming as she realized she was building up a sympathetic understanding with the teacher. She was very interested in poetry and

21

one day brought to me some she had written. I talked to her about blank verse and metre, length of lines, and the sound qualities of words and sent her off to look in anthologies for examples of this kind of poetry. She produced an excellent booklet, beautifully illustrated, showing the points we had talked about and, thus prepared, went off to write her own poetry. I had spoken about 'the right moment', using a stimulus, etc. and told her it might be several weeks before she was able to write some poetry. In fact, it was about a fortnight before she came with several poems in a booklet.

The Woods

As the breeze
Blew through the trees

I walked the woods
In silence.

The woods were clothed in snow

And the birds flew
And the wind blew

And all hands were aglow.

Bonfire Night

As golden leaves
Fall from the trees
The children realise
This time of year
It's Autumn time
And bonfire night is near

As children dance up round the fire
The flames they leap up, higher, higher,
Roman candles glitter bright
And rockets fly into the night.

And Think ...

A horse, a bird, a squirrel too
A tractor, dog and plough.

An oak, an ash, a stately yew
A farmer waiting now.

These things spell country
For me as I walk
And think ...

Something of the child's personality is reflected in these poems. The sensitive, reflective, rather solitary nature of this girl can be seen.

This work led to the study of a great poet—Christine chose Wordsworth, not surprisingly, because she had a great love of the countryside and its activities.

I asked her about the era of Wordsworth and poetry through the ages and suggested a time-chart as a possibility. She acted on this and looked up the periods of many poets and inserted them on a time-chart.

She came one day with a poem written out so as to resemble the drawing of a man. I suggested that it might be fruitful to look for other unusual or odd poems. This she did and enlisted the help of other children who came up with some interesting finds ... In the friendly, open atmosphere existing in this classroom, I always found it pleasing to note the ease with which children involved their friends in their own work. This practice sometimes led to group work and often became the starting point for other individual work by children whose interest had been first aroused by being brought in to help.

Christine went to the teacher one day with a Complete Works of Shakespeare. 'Most of the plays in here are nothing, only poetry. I don't understand them but I can tell they're poetry—they read like poetry anyway even though most of them have no rhymes.' I thought this was a very pertinent comment from a ten-year-old.

Sounds: my discoveries—John

John was a highly intelligent boy with a well developed reasoning power. He decided to make up a book on 'My discoveries about sound'. He had been browsing through the book shelf and picked up a typical junior school science book containing suggestions for experiments. Curiously enough, he used these suggestions only as a starting point. He had an original frame of mind and preferred to make up, observe, and record his own experiments. This I encouraged and was gratified to note that Barker (1965) draws the conclusion that, 'Perhaps it is in the fostering of the capacity for scientific thought, by the children discovering and checking facts for themselves and reporting on what they find, that the real value of the method lies.' Another point can be made here. I am not a scientist and in fact feel somewhat inadequate to deal with junior school science. I always thought, however, that the discovery table and challenge cards used in this classroom were a fine stimulus, leading to real personal discovery, wider experience, and consolidation of half-formed concepts. Barker seems to substantiate this as he says, 'It is clear that such is the interest among our young children that even the non-scientist can do a great deal merely by providing opportunities and encouragement.'

John noted for a day any sounds he heard—a remarkable list of over one hundred examples. He then described each sound after showing me the list: incidentally many of the staff became involved in helping to do this, especially the crossword fans.

In this booklet, John had a page on vibration and described several experiments he had tried. At the baths, the teacher rang a bell under water and the children could hear this under water. Here again we saw how the teacher extended an individual interest to bring in other children. In this way their interest was sparked off, perhaps to develop in another field. The topic, 'All at sea', briefly described later, developed from this same session at the baths through play in a dinghy which had previously been used in trying out some of John's experiments in sound.

Making unusual sounds led to making music with milk bottles containing varying amounts of water. 'I can't play the piano, sir, but I can play a tune on these—listen.'

The teacher turned the discovery table into a sound museum at this point and brought other children into the scheme as collectors, collators, arrangers, and recorders. This was a mark of very good teaching as he used children who needed this extra spur, recognition, and success in a new field. Tommy, a particularly difficult boy in an unfortunate home situation settled down quietly to work on his allotted task and continued afterwards to take other suggestions and try them out. As Susan Isaacs (1930) says, 'How quickly they respond to any opportunity which their environment offers for following out further the first movement of wonder and inquiry.' Tommy and John were poles apart in every way, but this common interest meant that John was soon instructing Tommy in the working of the tin can telephone. This situation was nurtured by the flexible, individually-geared organization of this classroom where creative thinking was both encouraged and rewarded.

John went on to test echoes and discovered (without any prompting at all) why echoes occurred. 'It's easy to make an echo in the sand hole (a disused quarry) near our house.' 'Why?' 'Because the sides are all fairly straight and the sounds bang back and forward making echoes.'

What John learned about sound was insignificant in comparison with the usefulness of the topic in helping him to form new, meaningful concepts and to solve problems by reasoning and deduction from the given data. It encouraged him to formulate the unknown from the known. Moreover, through the social interaction of helping himself and others, it became the means whereby he could see the difficulties of the other children in perceiving the relationships which were so obvious to him.

Wheels—David

David had been working on circular patterns and looking at the mathematical properties of circles. Seeing an infant playing with a spinning top one day, he decided to try to make one. This was fairly successful but here his interest started to flag. He had been playing with the tops he had made for some time when the teacher stepped in to ask about his work and how it was progressing. David said he thought he had come to a halt but that he had enough circular cut-outs to keep the class modellers going for weeks with wheels! Jokingly, he said he thought he might do some research on wheels. The teacher recorded this conversation and asked David to try to get himself organized quickly. The next entry shows that two days later, David was well under way with his work on wheels. The N.F.F. (1965) co-operative study scheme, 'Finding out Activities in the Primary School' suggests 'recording cases where some particular contribution seemed to mark a turning point or to make an important difference, e.g., some child's remark or question or special achievement, or some other happening which supplied new impetus, or caused a change of direction, or deepened or broadened the scope of an activity.' David's change of direction and the teacher's record illustrates this principle well, the work described, leading from the original, being far more creative, and generating deeper interest than the first starting point.

First he made a survey of the history of wheels. He recorded an experiment of dragging a load on a sledge and measured the effort required on a spring balance. He then pulled the same load on a small truck and compared the effort required, surely the best form of scientific discovery, arising from a basically historical piece of work.

David examined wheels and spokes and looked at the use of wheels in war (a subject that came into most of his work). Changing designs of wheels on transport through the ages was his next topic. He asked the class to see how many vehicles they could name which ran on wheels —this became a very long list.

He looked at unusual uses of wheels, because he had found a book dealing with this: water-wheels, wheels on paddle steamers, wheels in clocks, dials on telephones, wheels on winding gear in a coal mine, cog wheels on a machine, steering wheels on cars—the list seemed endless. He scorned a suggestion that a trundle wheel in the classroom might give him some ideas. 'They're always using it, I'll make another.' He brought a trundle wheel the following day made from a bicycle wheel. (Dad's handiwork was very evident, but nevertheless, David did make considerable effort himself in acquiring and subsequently using it.) One completely spontaneous activity stemming from this was a comparison of the number of revolutions between the school trundle and David's over a given distance. The teacher developed considerable mathematical experiences from this activity with a group of children which involved comparison of distances and revolutions. They also calculated ratio, and compared length of paces and the time taken to cover certain distances. Certainly, here is an example of a teacher raising levels of children's thinking through development of a spontaneous interest.

Other topics in outline

Many other topics were recorded during this period. A selection of the topics described here have been adapted and re-presented with a children's approach as discovery-learning situations. These are published by Thomas Hope & Sankey Hudson Ltd, under a general heading *To Point the Way* (J. Foster and D. B. Selby, 1966), Sets 1-6 (36 cards in all). Some of these are described very briefly here as an indication of the scope of the work and to show the pattern of children's personal discovery around an initial basic idea.

THEY HAVE HOMES TOO! This was a study of the homes of animals. The children studied most common animals and their habits and special names given to animal homes. They made a model of a squirrel's drey and were lucky enough to be able to observe the habits of a family of squirrels while staying in the countryside on a school journey. *The Wind in the Willows* proved to be a favourite with the children and led to creative expression in both modelling and writing. They arranged a special display of books about animals from the library and wrote their own stories. Looking after pets was a renewed interest stimulated by another study for this topic. An opportunity arose here to try to help children to look after their pets properly and to record details of the animals in their care.

LOGS, CANOES, AND CORACLES This work involved a study of man's first attempts to move on water, the making of stone-age boats. Two boys used their own models for experiments on floatation. Surprisingly enough, many of their own ships floated really well. We discussed boats both large and small and made comparisons between boats at various stages in history.

A CASTLE IN WALES An individual study arising from a holiday visit. The history of Harlech Castle, and the people connected with it, developed into a study of other similar Welsh castles and of the first Prince of Wales. The boy made models including flags and pennants. He reproduced these in large numbers and became absorbed in examining heraldic designs.

TELEPHONES One boy's interest in home-made telephones led on to work on the history of the telephone, the transatlantic cable, radio telephones, and satellites. He described the correct procedure for using a telephone and the intricacies of Subscriber Trunk Dialling in booklet form, and listed important local numbers, telephone charges, special services, and the location of local public telephones.

THE CONSTANT BATTLE   After a particularly bad storm and some local flooding, these things were the topic of some class discussion. Two children made booklets covering their inquiries into storm damage, erosion, deposition, dykes, and dredging. Other topics included work on the dangers caused by snow and ice on the roads, snow clearing schemes, the coastguard service, the lifeboat, and the gale warning systems.

LONDON'S BURNING   A television programme interested one boy in the Great Fire of London. His first enthusiasm, encouraged by the teacher, directed him to source material which led to booklets on the Great Fire, the London blitz, Samuel Pepys, fire insurance, Sir Christopher Wren, home safety and the prevention of fire, poster designs for fire danger and the principles on which fire extinguishers work. A visit to the fire station was arranged and some children wrote original stories.

ALL AT SEA   Stemming from a book of sea stories, this was the work of one boy from a family with nautical connections. His inquiries led him into the field of navigation, nautical terms and nautical mathematics, types of ships, and sea routes. The school subsequently took an interest in the work of the Ship Adoption Society.

FAMOUS BUILDINGS   This was the unaided work of one boy without any supervision. It seems that the initial interest stemmed from a visit to a cathedral made earlier. David, an intelligent boy with a streak of rugged individuality, had collected a mass of material on the topic of famous buildings. This included famous buildings of the past, important local buildings, and a quiz. He had also found pictures, postcards, book references, instructions for making models, and commercially-produced folders.

THE FLOODED VALLEY A first year junior class had worked on 'The story of tap water' and produced a colourful and instructive frieze. Brian had seen this and found it linked with an interest he was already pursuing, the making of a reservoir by flooding a valley. This reinforced his interest and subsequently, with advice, help and a lead from the teacher, he included in his booklet descriptions, drawings, and diagrams of water pumps, wells, reservoirs, water conservations, filtration, drains, artesian wells, household water systems, taps and washers, bursts, and a hot water system.

ANIMALS AT WORK A series of individual studies on a group theme. The group generally looked at the various working activities of animals round the world—both working for man and working for themselves. Each child took a particular animal and studied it. They brought their work together for a final display and discussion.

WAITING FOR THE TIDE Another topic arising out of a visit—this time a school trip to the seaside. Paul went on his annual holiday only a week after the school trip. He was able to follow-up many of the interests previously introduced. On his return, he classified his collection from the beach and rocks, presented tide tables and worked out problems from them, and made a model of a lighthouse. At this point, another group of children made a model of a harbour. Paul continued by writing a Punch and Judy play, writing about pleasure craft he had seen, and a lifeboat house he had visited.

THE SCHOOL BUS Many pieces of individual work were produced in connection with this study but by its very nature, co-operative effort was involved in some parts of the work, e.g., dramatic representation of the school bus with children playing the part of the conductor and other passengers. Timing buses also involved joint enterprise, as did the traffic census. There were, however, many individual studies, among the most successful of which were various mathematical schemes based on the school bus experiences. Children made up problems based on the timetable, they checked the times of various journeys, drew diagrams of bus-routes, and wrote stories, containing number work, which also described people making the journey.

Many other topics were carried out along these same lines. Although all were different in content and approach, they followed the same basic sequence as those described already: they involved a stimulus, an extension of a child's interest, and an evolving pattern, worked out by a child but guided where necessary by the teacher. These themes are examples of the topics covered by individual children in the period under review: Various animal studies; Cooking and baking; Water; Temperature; Natural measures; Handwriting; Ships; Trains; Tropical birds; Building; Manners; Clothing; Rooms; Growing things; Music making; Rainbows; Parcels and packages; Photography; String and rope; Tools; Stamps; Ballet; Boats; Aeroplanes; Horses; Shadows and reflections; Number stories; Excluding rain (umbrellas, rainwear); Lighting; Beautiful things; Making an instrument; Colour at night; Antiques.

Assignment cards

The whole concept of assignment cards in schools today is a thorny one. There are those who would not use them at all. They see them as an inhibiting factor in the child's own explorations, structuring his thinking, becoming a substitute for first-hand experience, and stultifying his approach. There are other teachers whose whole approach is based on a system of assignment cards. These teachers claim that they are an efficient system of providing an individual approach where the teacher's time is limited. I believe that there is a place for the assignment card in the discovery learning classroom, but I have seen work cards used in some classrooms as the very negation of active inquiry: where a whole class is working through a series of questions based on information given either on the card or in one book to which the card relates. This is, to my mind, a very formal approach and in no way encourages individual learning. Under this system, the child is fitted to the card. It is the card which becomes the principal component of the learning, the child is relegated to the role of unthinking recorder, selector in many cases of the right response from a multiple choice type of answer. Used in this way, as a blanket approach, these cards have no place in progressive primary schools. I believe, however, that there is a place for an ordered approach which the child can use to begin a line of inquiry. A good assignment card, correctly introduced by an astute teacher, can help to do this.

One of the usual characteristics of this technique is that it is formulated beforehand. The cards may be commercially produced or made by the teacher. There is a long educational history of assignment cards, evolving from questions at the end of each chapter in old textbooks, through a 'things to do' phase, again usually after each chapter, and on to the formation of activity books and work books sometimes associated with a given approach or set of books. In fact, the very question of what to call the aid presents a problem. Assignment cards, work cards, things to do, question books, ideas to follow up, all describe this prepared material. None of these seems to me to describe adequately the help which the good aid should give. Having used the titles, 'Pointer cards', 'Research notes' and 'Fresh fields booklets', I have come to the conclusion that the name is unimportant so long as the children know how they are to be used, understand their function, and respect their limitations.

One teacher collected a wide variety of assignment cards in the classroom and evolved an efficient catalogue system so that they were easily identified under a cross reference system. Cards the teacher had made were then incorporated and used when they became relevant. There is no such thing as the perfect assignment card. The most a teacher can hope for is that it will be possible to provide a card which most nearly fits the requirements of a particular child when he needs help.

Students in colleges of education on teaching practice in primary schools are often aghast when a child comes along and asks for information on a topic about which the student is quite ignorant. The starting point for primary school children's interests is often outside the scope of the teacher. This is one instance where an assignment card could be useful. The very organization of a whole class for individual work can present a grave problem for the inexperienced teacher, who may find prepared material useful. This needs to be carefully selected, vetted, and supervised. Continual guidance and support will be required throughout and the pitfalls already noted borne in mind.

In general, I would look for the following points in a commercially produced assignment card or attempt to include these points in any cards I was producing myself: the card should contain ideas which encourage the child to think and produce his own ideas for development of the topic. There should be encouragement for the child to seek information from many different sources, to compare findings, and assess any differences noted. The use of a variety of material should be urged and expression of results should be encouraged in many different forms. Appeal should be made to many senses and an emphasis placed on the value of first-hand experience. Ideas should be realistic but should not be entirely classroom based; a link should be established between out-of-school activities and the work on hand in school. Collection of materials should be encouraged and help given with initial ideas for sorting and classifying. Where information may be difficult to trace, an introduction of this on the card may be desirable and some help given as to where to find additional material. Diagrams, plans, and simple illustrations may be effective. Some note should be taken of the reading level: is it easily read by slow readers? Will slow readers require help initially? Can other children give this help or must the teacher give it? The card should contain ideas for further study, leading on from the basic theme of the card to other related areas of work.

Given these bases for using assignment cards, the teacher might use them as a prepared lead, to give individually the guidance which it must be acknowledged would ideally be given on a personal basis. Used astutely, cards of this type can assist both the teacher and the child when classes are large.

3

Children learning by discovery
in groups

The group studies described here show the development of activities with groups of children of varying ages. The work was carried out by students. Some of it took place in schools as part of their teaching practice and involved a student working informally with a small group of children. Some studies took place at home with small groups around the house. These are included to show that the pattern of learning is often the same in school and at home if the conditions are such that the child can 'find out' and extend interests and natural curiosities. A unique feature is that the groups involved children of a wide age range working together.

I have analysed two of these group schemes in detail: 'The telephone' and 'Homes and housebuilding'. The outline of six additional schemes will show briefly how children took an original stimulus and extended it according to their interest and inclination. All schemes described here show the branching out which will occur when children are given the opportunity to think and act creatively, use their imagination, and tackle problems inventively.

The telephone

Children: David, aged fourteen years; Margaret, aged eight years; Steven, aged five years.

STARTING POINT   Three old telephone receivers obtained cheaply from the G.P.O., a model of a public telephone box, reference books on telephones, a simple book the teacher had made on the construction of telephones and the telephonic communication system, telephone directories, a 'tin can and string' telephone, a baby-alarm, a money-box for calls which was commercially produced and suitably inscribed.

DEVELOPMENT   David, who had a mechanical frame of mind, immediately started to dismantle one of the telephones. He found out how the bell worked and examined the carbon microphone (the interest here stemmed from a school chemistry lesson). He assembled a wide selection of tools to help him to do this job and was quite selective in their use. Margaret immediately began dramatic play with a telephone. She dialled 999 and asked the police to remove a madman from the attic stairs. She monopolized the 'phone—taking imaginary messages on a pad and charging up the cost of her calls. The first reaction of Steven was, 'We have some NEW telephones.' He was then disappointed that no one answered and that the 'phones were rather old and battered. He rang the police and reported a lion in the cellar. He threw himself into this fantasy to the extent that he put on his cowboy suit and gun belt and stationed himself at the top of the cellar stairs, making little runs back to the telephone to report progress in the capture of the lion. The value of play and the egocentric orientation at five years of age is well illustrated by this example.

Steven was also interested in the model telephone box and expressed a desire to make a similar model. He did this using a shoe box and lots of red paint. There was no suggestion of working with the others. He had obviously not yet reached the age of needing the socialization offered by the group situation. This is borne out by Sprott (1958), who says, 'By the age of six and seven years more stable groups appear—or can appear if space and opportunity are offered. When this happens the social learning we call give and take begins.' I would like to emphasize Sprott's accent on 'space and opportunity' because on the occasion when these were available, Steven soon became interested in working with Margaret. They both went outside. Margaret wished to use the 'tin-can' telephone but needed a partner for this. She gave Steven his instructions and with the motivation of novelty and excitement of participation and sense of achievement he was soon happily playing with Margaret.

A fire on the hillside opposite started David thinking about systems of warning before the telephone—about beacons and passing messages from hill-top to hill-top. The children remembered the site of an ancient beacon they had seen during holidays. They then discussed other methods of passing messages: Red Indians' smoke signals, tapping messages through walls, flag waving, morse code, drumming, bell ringing. Margaret asked Steven to go into an adjoining room and she tapped on the wall to him. He tapped back but could not repeat a rhythm. This led on to dramatic play about Robin Hood being imprisoned and arranging an escape. (Here Steven gave the impression of enjoying his part quite independently of Margaret, an example of the parallel nature of his play at this time.) Children at this stage illustrate all types of play stages within a few minutes.

One important aspect of this study is that it shows clearly the way in which drama becomes spontaneous given the right stimulus. A telephone seems just the right provision for this. David was interested in telling the other children about telephones in police-cars and taxis. The children listened with what appeared to be polite interest, then soon wanted to go out to make a bonfire to see if smoke signals really worked.

The difference in the ages of the children did seem to enlarge the scope of possibilities of the original stimulus. The most significant fact emerging for me is that such a technical-seeming object as the telephone can be of such absorbing interest for a five-year-old—and how inventive he was. Who but a five-year-old would have discovered the joy of dialling with his toes!

Homes and housebuilding

Children: Christopher, aged six years; Sharon, aged eight years; Denise, aged eight years.

STARTING POINT The following items connected with housebuilding were displayed: samples of cement, sand, hardcore, different kinds of brick, a breeze block, wood, hardboard, blockboard, copper piping, glass, nails, screws, tiles, slate, asbestos sheeting, lead, plaster, charts showing different kinds of houses, a chart showing some house construction, a house plan, reference books.

DEVELOPMENT The children first looked at the material, identified most of it easily, and were able to tell about its place in the house. 'Daddy used tiles like these to mend the kitchen roof.' 'These screws are a lot bigger than those in my Meccano.'

Plastic guttering and drainpipes puzzled them, but when they examined a rusted metal gutter and compared the two, they agreed plastic had the advantage in being rust-free.

'We haven't any glass like this in our house, but we've lots of other sorts. Let's count how many different kinds of glass we can find.' (They found eleven kinds.)

They looked at the books and saw the challenge cards with them. 'Which kind of house do you live in?' They decided to write about their own homes and this soon extended to other homes. 'Cave men' was a popular choice and gave rise to much searching through books, reading, and discussion. Sharon's mother is German so she wrote about 'Houses in other lands', having recently been abroad. Her account of her trips broadened the discussion considerably and the group were soon busy discussing airports, ships, foreign railways, flats in Germany, and foreign foods. Sharon taught the others several German words. I came to the conclusion that the 'direct method' must be a natural one as Sharon used it perfectly in her lesson.

Christopher significantly was not interested in houses of long ago or houses of other lands. His interests were, as we might expect, nearer home. He wished to build his own house and went into the garden to set some bricks (left by the builder). Told to look at how the bricks had been laid in the house wall, he soon copied the pattern. The following day they seized on a book about animal houses. The girls wanted to read this, but Christopher interrupted to tell them about Noah's Ark which they were making at school.

The children were familiar with the work at a local brick yard and soon wanted to make some bricks. Luckily it was possible to take this interest in two directions. First, they made a sand, cement, and hardcore mixture and used a small hand brick-making machine to turn out some concrete block type bricks. We then discussed how normal house bricks are made and compared the two. Secondly, the children decided to make some model bricks out of clay and let them dry. They did this and built a small hut several days later using real mortar to set their bricks. Christopher could not shape his bricks accurately and was soon in trouble with the girls who thought his bricks might spoil the house. (His bricks were coming out square.) He was just on the point of giving up when he cut his brick down the centre and ended up with two bricks of the right shape. He did this accidentally, but soon recognized that the two halves were the correct proportion, 'Look I can make two at once.'

He continued this with great success. The girls ignored his discovery and carried on making their individual oblong bricks even though they now saw the other method to be quicker. Perhaps the 'discovery' must essentially be one's own at this age for it to be used or perhaps they didn't like to admit that a younger child had found a better method. After a while, however, he was paid the compliment of 'Your bricks are a bit better now, aren't they?'

Estimation of the length of the room arose out of the building of the model hut. They guessed at six feet and eight feet. They seemed to count the number of widths of wallpaper and convert these into feet. They enjoyed the actual measuring and their ability to estimate distance did improve.

These three children for the most part worked individually—the group aspect came from comparisons of their individual efforts. The best example of co-operation and social 'give and take' was in making the model, using the children's own bricks. It was here that each had different ideas to contribute. Sharon seemed to guide the progress, often giving direct orders which were at first somewhat resented, then later passively accepted. Sprott (1958) emphasizes this when he says 'Every group involves emotional relations of like and dislike among its members, it develops norms of its own, and it develops a hierarchy of prestige often culminating in a single person who has a dominating influence.'

The joy of discovery comes out very clearly in some of the examples as does the suitability of group work, for children of junior school age. Ash and Rapaport (1960) report, 'Much of the work done in the junior school is organised in groups because ... juniors are at the gang stage ... and some things are best taught to a group who have reached a certain stage.' Although no conscious effort was made to teach 'skills' in these schemes, the opportunity for teaching arose out of a need for a skill to carry forward an interest. Skills learned in this way will most likely be learned with insight: this learning will also be secure and a good foundation for future learning.

One other point to emerge clearly from this work is that as a general rule, the examples bear out accepted principles: that it is more at junior school level that children make the social adjustments necessary for group work. Although children in the five to seven age group work 'in' the group situation, they are not 'of' it.

Other topics in outline

The following six additional group schemes are given in outline to show the scope of the work, its starting point, the children involved, and the areas covered. Generally speaking, they follow the same principles as those analysed in detail. They are suggestions for source material, stimuli which practising teachers and students may find useful as a basis for adaptation in their own work.

NAILBOARD   The children: Two boys, aged six and eight years, and a girl aged nine years.

Starting point: various squares of pegboard and nailboard, elastic bands, a variety of cardboard shapes, coloured, gummed paper.

Development: all the children painted abstract patterns. They discovered and used figures of many sides, e.g., triangle, rectangle, octagon. The boys made pictures with elastic bands on the nailboard. They followed this by making models of ships. They pulled the ships along the ground and studied friction and the use of wheels. The girl worked on area, made up problems and solved them practically, using the nailboard. The children cut out shapes, made on the nailboard, in card, and used these to make pictures. They all made letters on the nailboard and the eight-year-old wrote a book about this. George made angles on his pegboard and learned to measure these using a protractor. He continued by making maps and using a compass to chart directions. Finally, the nailboard became part of the standard play equipment of the six-year-old.

A CUP OF TEA   The children: Lesley, aged thirteen years (average ability); Tony, aged nine years (high ability); Kay, aged eight years (above average ability).

Starting point: tea samples showing the stages in its preparation from growing leaf to the tea used at home, a cup, saucer, teapot, milk jug and plate in pottery and china, a globe with tea-growing areas marked, pictures of tea plantations and pickers, poems about tea, samples of tea from packets, some perfumed tea and tea bags, a magnifying glass, a tea caddy, empty packets, several booklets about tea, a collection of library books.

Development: the children weighed samples and played shop. They were interested in new words, e.g., blend, caddy, package, clipper. Creative activities developed. Lesley used tea in a collage picture and Kay used it in a design. They cut up packets, used tea bags to paint and tea as a dye. They wrote about tea and tried to describe the taste of several different varieties. 'Tea-time' led to a study of telling the time and time zones. They compared time in the tea-growing regions and England. Tony looked up details of the clipper ships, wrote down his findings, and drew the ships. They found out how much tea was carried by some ships, calculated how many hundredweight bags this would fill, and estimated how many cups of tea could be made from a shipload. They examined the designs on china cups, discussed the willow pattern, and made finger pots in clay. Kay collected cards from packets of tea. Lesley made a booklet called 'Food we like' which was an extension of the interest in tea.

WEIGHING   The children: John, aged six years; Charles, aged five years; Anne, aged eight years.

Starting point: an antique pair of scales (made of brass and very beautiful), a home-made balance, a large balance with a pointer fixed at the fulcrum, a spring balance, letter scales, scales with balancing pans and weights, an equalizing balance, bathroom scales.

Development: sensory experiences predominated at first. The group just felt the scales and balances. They pushed, pressed, lifted, swayed, watched, and tested the movements. They rushed to weigh articles and spent time finding suitable ones. They collected an enormous assortment. At the teacher's suggestion that it might be possible to do some cooking, they weighed ingredients, looked at recipes, recorded what they had done and used the cakes for buying and selling as well as eating. They weighed money and watched money being weighed on a visit to the bank. They talked about how unusual it was to weigh money instead of counting it. The teacher helped Anne to make a histogram as she weighed various articles. They weighed each other and the teacher, recorded their results, and then began measuring heights. The others joined in with Anne eventually to make histograms.

THE SEASHORE   The children: Tony, Beryl, Pat, Maureen; all aged six to seven years and about average ability.

Starting point: arranged on a tray to simulate a seashore were shells, sand, rocks, starfish, seahorse, seaweed, driftwood, sand-dune grass, nets, model boats.

Development: the children examined the display. There was lots of discussion and recapitulation of holiday experiences. An interest in textures evolved. The girls described the feel of several articles and Tony copied out the words which the teacher had listed, before adding to the list itself. They made patterns by using the shells. They made lines in the sand with their hands and commented on the pattern they had formed. Drawing and painting followed these activities. An interest in shapes developed and they drew spirals, cones, fan-shaped shells, and stars. They enjoyed counting the shells and sorting them into groups. Tony experimented with the shells and found those that floated. The girls joined in and divided them into hard and soft, brittle and flexible, and smooth and rough. An interest in collecting was encouraged. They borrowed and examined an elder sister's collection of shells, and determined to look for more types. 'Isn't this beautiful', said Beryl holding up a shell. They made a booklet containing pictures of 'The beautiful things around us'. The teacher compared this interest with that reported by Susan Isaacs at Malting House. There was great interest in the physical world and natural phenomena in this group.

TEXTURE   The children: Carolyn, aged five years; Elizabeth, aged six years; Judith, aged eleven years.

Starting point: rubber, lace, wool, fur, washers, stones, polythene, coal, coke, peat, metals, plastic, paper, loofah, shells, nuts, twigs, bark, wire, pottery, vegetables, cloth.

Development: the first approach was to classify the display. This was especially interesting because of the varying approaches of the children and was an indication of their different developmental levels. They experimented to see if items floated. They divided them into edible and inedible, etc. They brought other items to add to the collection, which they listed. Judith placed these in alphabetical order. She also described the feel of the articles in a writing book she used for other interests. They made a collage with some of the materials. The teacher reported that this followed a similar pattern to one attempted earlier in the week. Judith requested that the teacher should make word cards to match the articles. They made up a game in which they matched cards and items.

CARS   The children: Alan, aged nine years; James, aged ten years; Robert, aged twelve years.

Starting point: the boys all had a strong interest in cars, and the items available were a large-scale model of a Morris 1100, a hub cap and tyre from a car, many scale-model cars on a model road setting, the highway code, some road maps, reference books on cars, publicity leaflets on cars, a foot pump, night driving glasses, a sun visor, an elliptical headlight glass, a parking light, various other appropriate bric-à-brac.

Development: they began with a game of finding the route. One boy gave the starting and finishing point, another found the route, and the third boy checked its suitability. They drew cars, mostly copying from publicity leaflets, but paying great attention to detail. Robert asked for a compass to use in route finding and spent a long time experimenting with this. James made a simple compass using a school science book as a guide. Robert worked out lines of force with iron filings. They made a model of a car—simple chassis and axles with a body built on. The teacher showed them some pictures of veteran cars. The boys had a surprisingly accurate knowledge of when motoring began. They wrote books on the early years of motoring which included interviews with two people who remembered motoring before 1914. A map of the world produced late in the study led to marking oil-producing countries, rubber-producing countries, and indicating the countries to which one large firm exported vehicles.

A comparison of two groups of children learning by discovery

Two groups of children, aged ten and eleven years, were shown: a book giving specifications of ships, holiday cruise brochures, a list of ships sailing from Southampton, cuttings from newspapers about the QE2. Group A had IQ scores ranging from 128 to 136 while the IQ scores of group B ranged from 80 to 96. The student carrying out this study observed the children closely and discussed problems with the groups. The aim was to study the way the groups reacted to the stimulus and to try to identify examples of creative problem solving and imaginative development stemming from the starting point provided.

Both groups worked out mathematical problems, made models, drew ships, examined geographical ideas, and wrote imaginatively about ships, cruises, and islands. The most interesting point which emerged from this study concerned group A, the high intelligence group. There were clear indications that these children needed a situation where they could extend their knowledge and experience. They needed activities which provided a real challenge to their intellect. They used adult study methods and acquired information easily from encyclopedias and reference books, using economical ways of selecting relevant facts. They made up problems, designed assignment cards for others, checked them, and amended them. They thought out new activities quickly and maintained a prolific output. Their own satisfaction in success led them to strive for new goals, something which was never noticed in the less able group.

These characteristics show the need for the teacher constantly to challenge and stimulate able children. The children had read *Treasure Island* and knew the principles of ordnance survey contours and making relief maps. They commented on mountainous districts in Scotland and Wales when studying a map, and said in comparison that Anglesey was 'only hilly'. They saw the reasons for Southampton and Liverpool developing into great ports. One boy suggested they make a map of Arran. The teacher gave them plasticine in five colours. Peter said, 'We can use a layer for each contour and build up the hills in various colours.' He added, 'We can then slice the mountain of Goatfell and see the different layers.' Andrew replied that 'this would only show contours; if we had more information on the mountain, we could make the colours represent different layers of rock.' Clearly, children thinking at this level need activities which are intellectually demanding. The teacher who fails to recognize the tremendous potential of the highly gifted young child and to cater for it can rightly be criticized. This group made a model of the course of a river. Sally reported, 'We made some rivers by running our pencils down the sides of the mountains and then finding an eye-dropper and dropping some water down at the top so that it looked real.' Following this they solved engineering problems when the plain became flooded. They widened the river bed as it approached the sea and noticed that the water appeared to travel faster at the top of the mountain and more slowly when the river widened. The problems discussed here are similar to those faced by civil engineers and yet these children could identify the difficulties and suggest ways of overcoming them.

The main difference in the way these two groups reacted to the stimulus was the ability of group A to apply principles far better than group B. Also, once they had begun, group A followed up any idea with vigour, quickly developing any thread of the topic which attracted them. Group B had less ability to work as a group. They needed much more individual attention and required personal starting points for their work. They were unable to take the ideas provided for the group and find something to begin alone, probably because of a lack of initiative, drive, and originality. The student also noticed a hesitancy, lack of confidence, poor use of language, immature aesthetic appreciation, and more need for the basic security of love and affection in the less able children.

4

Children learning by discovery
as a class

I have already indicated the usefulness of complexity and novelty in the learning situation. In general school routine, I often felt that the classes needed a complete change of direction, a re-channelling of their efforts, a move away from school itself in some cases, and at the same time, a scheme which would have a socializing effect on the class; making them aware of their group responsibilities. It was with these thoughts in mind that the staff decided that each term, the class would carry out a class scheme which would endeavour to fulfil these aims.

I shall describe one of these schemes, 'A Treasure Hunt', which was carried out with a fourth year unstreamed class. Another scheme, 'The School Census', is a further example of this type of work, and I have noted briefly about a dozen other schemes.

A treasure hunt

I make no apology for the fact that this first scheme was

not originated by the children. I searched for an idea which would appeal strongly to top juniors and make them think carefully, solve problems, reason logically, and take decisions based on their findings. Bartlett (1958) says, 'These forces which lie behind the human zest for adventure are continually revolting against, and breaking out of the closed system.' Here is the force we must harness and channel towards productive, adventurous thinking. 'Always,' says Bartlett, 'he [the teacher] must try to use the information that is available to him so as to reach a terminus based upon that information, but not identified with it.' In the structuring of the treasure hunt we tried to cater for this situation, to take children outside school, and give them real problems to solve. Too often, school is an island, unrelated to the world outside where people spend most of their time thinking, reasoning, and being at some stage of involvement with a problematic set of circumstances. Hollamby (1962) points out that, 'A young child learns most through his own experiments and explorations ... he needs freedom and opportunity to explore his environment, for it is the impact of these first hand experiences which is so valuable.' A treasure hunt, outside the immediate confines of the school, seemed to us to be a very exciting prospect for top juniors.

We divided the children into groups of varying academic ability, with four or five boys and girls in each group. A group leader was appointed by the children themselves. The groups began work at ten minute intervals, starting at 10 a.m. They returned at about 3 p.m. and discussed the day's activities before going home.

Some clues were such that finding the answer to one gave them another clue, but we divided the whole venture into twenty sections, some containing three or four clues. Marks were awarded for each section, so that if a group had trouble with a particular clue it did not prejudice their overall chances. Sections could be tackled in any order, with the exception of the last one which brought them back to school to make a short written report before handing in their papers. Afterwards, we gave another simple clue which enabled them to collect a small box of 'treasure' each and wait for the return of the other groups for summing-up and the announcement of the results.

Each group was given 15p at the beginning of the hunt and had to account for any money spent. They left school on geographical directions and a plan involving some very simple map reading. Next came a clue in rhyme to be picked up from a willing shopkeeper and an answer in rhyme was required.

The groups were asked to collect such diverse items as an old halfpenny, certain leaves, weeds, a cork of more than one inch in diameter, a theatre ticket, a horseshoe, and an article made by a firm holding a Royal Warrant. The children took a brass rubbing after unravelling one clue and a bark rubbing after another before finding four articles which they could label showing the name in French. Sketching salient points from buildings and road signs, and visiting the library to find answers to several questions were also included in the instructions. Work on three bus time-tables displayed in the area meant a lot of arithmetic before finally arriving at a number which was used in the next clue to give an address where a further clue was waiting. The children also went to the station to gather data to use in the calculation of fares, times, and distances. One section involved the use of the telephone to find the answer to one clue and receive another. Here again we had no shortage of helpers. We included some questions without comment or explanation just to see how the children would tackle them.

We tried to ask questions which would take the children into a type of place they would not normally visit and use subjects with which they would not normally be familiar. One question of this type introduced children to finding how a cheque is used, another to setting a place for dinner, and a third to examining a passport. A little formal grammar was brought in with a clue which had to be punctuated correctly before it was intelligible. Teachers could be consulted during the day on a point connected with the assignment sheet only at a cost of one bonus mark. Sometimes this was worthwhile as it could mean completing a section correctly and this could carry five marks.

We tried to keep to friendship patterns in the groups as far as possible, but gave no instructions at all regarding leadership. In all groups, a leader emerged fairly quickly but not always the child one would have expected. Many of the assignments were of a practical nature and in two of the groups, practical-minded children seemed to take charge even though there were some more academically able in the group. The natural organizers were very much to the fore in all groups. The children themselves selected the most appropriate leader and seemed content to follow once the scheme was underway. There was one group in which several children were potential leaders and in this group there was a certain amount of bickering. It is significant to record that this group had most consultations with the teacher and were bottom in the overall classification at the end of the day.

The winning group, when I looked carefully afterwards

at its composition, showed clearly that apart from working smoothly and cohesively together, this group contained children who had a high degree of social adaptation and a high level of communication. Both these factors were very necessary to be successful in this scheme. This fact would link up with Luria's (1961) findings that 'The development of the ability of the human being to control and order his own behaviour is in the strictest sense dependent on the development of the speech function.' Donaldson (1963) also makes a similar observation and shows that children who cannot talk freely have difficulty in limiting themselves to a problem. This point would seem to apply to one least successful group in this scheme.

I had wondered about the place of the dull child in this scheme. Would he be a passenger? Would the brighter children do all the thinking and solve all the problems? With these thoughts in mind, I had structured many of the activities to give the less academically inclined children a chance to shine. In fact, from what I could observe— and observation was difficult in this situation—the less able children were fairly well to the fore in any group decisions which had to be made. I thought eventually that these situations had, in fact, given these children a more practical problem that enabled them to think more objectively. Morris (1951) says that with dull children 'The aim must not be to steer the child clear of anything that savours of abstract thought but rather to encourage him at every turn to formulate his own abstractions from his own increasing understanding.' Perhaps the learning situations as seen in this treasure hunt did just this for these slower children.

Many children showed great initiative. To save money for bus fares, Ann did not use the public telephone but went home to use their own telephone because she wouldn't have to pay. Michael rang the Town Clerk's office to get information about council committee chairmen because it was cheaper than the bus fare to the Town Hall.

The section where several general questions were given without comment or explanation was interesting. It was here that the children who could think deeply about a problem scored. They had in one question to make a simple sketch map putting six well-known places in the area on to the map, making sure that the places were in the correct relationship to each other. This meant taking known information and setting it down as a related whole. If we take Bartlett's (1958) definition of understanding, 'The ability to reformulate what one "knows" in alternative terms, and the ability to use it in one's own thoughts and actions', we can see that this particular problem was asking the children to do just this. The results here were very good, but a similar question, asking them to do the same thing with surrounding towns proved to be too difficult. Obviously they did not have the same meaningful cognitive map of the area fifteen miles around their home as they had of the village itself.

I had taken no account of the follow-up activities, preferring to wait and see what effects this scheme had on the later work of the children. The effect was two-fold. First, for several weeks afterwards, everyone in school was a budding organizer of treasure hunts. Second, some of the suggested areas of work connected with the hunt were taken up afterwards as subjects for further study. Amongst these were: writing poetry, map drawing, bark rubbing, telephones, local government and bus routes. The scheme did have a boosting effect on the general application of the class to work in school. The party which was a natural consequence of the finding of the 'treasure' was also a great social occasion, referred to on many subsequent occasions.

A school census

Some notes of the activities of a class working on this scheme.

Starting point: the national census came up in general discussion. The teacher talked about this and gave background information. The class, being used to having to help to organize a class scheme about once a term, suggested that 'A School Census' might be the right topic for that particular term. This seemed a good idea and the work progressed.

Development: After the initial discussion there was a class meeting to decide on the plan. They decided how they would organize the census and what they would try to find out. Here are some of the subjects covered.

Each child answered a short questionnaire covering his attitude towards school milk and school meals. Every child in school was asked the following questions: (a) Have you a cycle? (b) How do you come to school? (c) What is your favourite television programme? (d) What is your favourite pop group? (e) How many hours a week do you spend watching television?

All the children in school were measured for height and weighed. The results were analysed and presented graphically. Fourth year junior children wrote about the results and tried to interpret their significance. An inventory of articles in school was made, each class being responsible for a different aspect.

The work necessitated a great deal of moving about

and co-operation with other classes. All the classes provided information, which was collected daily when necessary. Taking a school inventory certainly kept less able children very busy at tasks which they were able to enjoy —mostly counting and recording. As the information came in, it was sorted, and groups of children were given responsibility for dealing with each section. The 'glamour' of the scheme rubbed off on other classes who began to chart their own information as it was gathered in their class. This shows clearly how much a class scheme breaks down into individual and group assignments at one end of the scale and how it becomes a whole school concern at the other. The essence of all the work I would have considered fairly successful was that apart from being individually satisfying, it also contributed to the work of other children and to the tone of the school generally.

Other class schemes organized on these lines included: 'May Day'—a scheme based around May Day culminating in dancing round a Maypole; 'Machines'—a study covering machines of every type; 'The village survey'—a local studies scheme; 'High flats'—some high flats that were being built close by; 'The river near school'—the river used as a centre for field study; 'The supermarket'—a break-down of the working of the supermarket and its products; 'The world of grown-ups'—a wide scheme trying to answer children's questions about some of the problems which adults face in their everyday life; 'Manchester airport'—a visit with suitable preparation and follow-up activities; 'Colour and texture'—colour and texture used as a stimulus for creative writing; 'Flags'—basically art and design, the theme developed as the historical aspect opened up (heraldry and the use of flags for signalling were salient features of the work); 'Arranging a class party'—using the party as a means to introduce committee work, functions of officers, minutes, etc.

Objects and materials for use on classroom interest tables

AN INTRODUCTION I have shown how individual topics, group topics, and class topics link together. Sometimes individuals see common aims in their inquiries and join together, and groups come together as a class for joint ventures. The reverse is also true; that class units break down into groups and individuals. In the classroom, many of these studies, at all levels, originate from a 'growth point' provided on an interest table.

Examples of objects and materials which can be used on interest tables are given below under selected headings. The attention of the reader is drawn to classroom work described throughout the book, much of which is based on themes. Perusal of these schemes will provide lists of stimuli for use on interest tables for most of the topics described. Here, selected topics are highlighted as examples. Similar lists can be constructed by the reader for the topics described in the book simply by reading the account and noting down the objects and materials which were used. A study of chapters two and three will locate many suitable lists and themes.

TRANSFORMATIONS This is a fascinating topic for young children because changes are actually illustrated on the interest table. The objects can be wide-ranging as general stimulation, or deliberately kept to one group of materials for more specific work. Transformations can be grouped under headings; e.g. food, natural materials, personal care, manufacture, clothes etc. Many of these categories are inclusive of each other but if selection is desired, these groupings and many others can be considered. Among objects illustrating transformations which I have seen recently were these: natural stone/carved stone; clay/pottery; wood/furniture; coal/by-products; fruit/drinks; fur/hat; coffee beans/ground and instant coffee; seeds/germinated shoots; wool/sweater; article (dirty)/similar article (clean). Also various before/after pictures were used to show garden, face and environmental transformations.

PARCELS AND PACKAGES A selection of these items can be used: examples of commercial packaging; commercial packages opened up to show the basic design; examples of many ways in which parcels are fastened (e.g. glue, Sellotape, string, tape, staples, hooks, folding, flaps, pre-stressed pull mechanisms etc.); natural packages—eggs, skins, cocoons; pre-pressed, moulded packages; bottles; plastic containers; sachets; insulated containers; tins; pictures of barrels, haulage container units, tankers, etc.; picture of an airline meal, frozen dinner, and other convenience packaged foods.

The leads for study which may come from this display are endless. I have seen inquiries into almost every traditional subject generated from these articles.

COOKING AND BAKING Scales; specimen recipes on cards; cookery books; essential cooking ingredients; easily obtainable, possible ingredients; suggestions cards pointing out: (a) different ways in which ingredients could be used (encourage pupils to think of others), (b) basic transformations (link with earlier topics) which occur when commodities are mixed, (c) the use of estimation in cooking, and some of its effects, (d) clues to look for in avoiding possible failures; measuring jugs; measuring spoons; specimen utensils illustrating their suitability for different culinary processes; poster—first aid in the kitchen; instruction books for cookers: (a) gas, (b) electric; examples of kitchen equipment; report from a pupil on, 'A visit to the school kitchen'; sample menus from school; a menu from a restaurant; an example of place-setting; flour samples; yeast sample; poster showing examples of proteins, carbohydrates etc.; refrigeration instruction book; a comparison of costs between a convenience food item and its natural equivalent.

STRING AND ROPE Examples of different kinds of string and rope; string and rope mounted in interesting shapes and coils; uses of string and rope—examples in pictures —lists for pupils to add their own ideas; rope—stripped down to show coiling and how it is made; rope and string substitutes; reference books.

ANTIQUES I have used this topic as a starting point with several classes. It is an excellent open-ended stimulus, the objects providing the lead to a bewildering variety of topics. I suggest a simple beginning with several personal items to elicit interest. Soon, children bring items and the dialogue begins as a range of objects is built up, each with its own story.

COLOUR This can be approached by highlighting any primary colour, and collecting a mixture of objects and materials of that colour. So a red display, or a yellow display, etc., may be built up. The arrangement should be tastefully presented, and aesthetically pleasing. Use of drapes enhances a display. The colour can be changed after a time or the objects added to or exchanged. A blue display may contain: a variety of blue cloth; blue pottery, tinted glass, flowers, china, porcelain, ink, dye, candle, wallpaper etc.; a predominantly blue painting; articles dyed blue.

5

Children learning by discovery
as a school

The sense of belonging to 'the school', pride in the building, the other children, the teachers and the work, was something we always tried to encourage. Many writers of educational texts show the need for the school to have close links with the neighbourhood, to provide real-life learning situations, and to act as a base from which children can extend their inquiries into the widening world as it unfolds for them. Few of these writers dwell sufficiently, however, on the need to build up the sense of 'belonging', the feeling of joy in being a member of the whole school. If this feeling is encouraged, the school will have a greater and more lasting influence on the children who experience this affinity with the overall pattern of co-operation and help which should characterize our schools. When this has happened, we will, in the words of Mays (1962), be able to 'assist the youngsters to overthrow the cramping walls of their environment and to feel at times their pulses race with the tonic of adventure and the thrill of the unknown'.

It was with these thoughts in mind that the ideas of an

all-school project were first conceived. The general aims of the scheme were as follows: all the school should co-operate in the same scheme. Everyone should have the benefit of the same initial stimulus; and that this should be the point of growth from which every child and class should develop. The initial stimulus would develop differently in each class. Children would work at their own level at tasks suitable to their developmental stage and maturation.

The choice of a theme was something of a problem and it was only after much thought that we decided to organize a balloon race on the lines usually followed at fairs and garden fetes, but with this difference, that we harnessed the effort to provide each class with a source of study lasting for about a fortnight.

The balloon race—an all-school project

We began with a staff discussion on the merits of the scheme, followed by a period during which each teacher thought of possible provisions to be made for his/her class so that the children could branch out to lines of study which interested them. At this time, there were three infant and four junior classes in school. I shall first give a general picture of the lines of development in each year.

In the reception class there were many paintings showing the children releasing their balloons, with suitable captions for reading practice. Some collage work was attempted with scraps and fabrics, with very gay results. The teacher made books containing simple sentences describing the children's work and illustrated with collected pictures, photographs, and the children's own paintings.

Handling balloons in the classroom (not containing hydrogen, of course) gave rise to lots of number work, and before long these balloons were bought and sold in the shop. The wall story, children's individual writing, and the daily news-sheet were also concerned with balloons and, naturally, the five-year-olds were eager to talk about the work.

In the six-year-old class, much of the work took the same form as in the reception class, but at a different level. The children made number books based on the balloon study and there was opportunity for identifying colours, comparing balloons and their texture, and lots of interest in odd-shaped balloons and balloon sculpture. The top infant class carried out a variety of other ideas as well. Frieze work done by several groups showed balloons over the sea, mountains, forests, and towns. Cut-out balloons provided the basis for number work when they were arranged on the windows with name tags. Some work on foreign stamps and their countries of origin followed a suggestion that the balloons might reach another land. The children made maps and calculated distances and from this, an interest in travel literature grew.

In the first-year junior class, the children suggested much of the line of action. An interest in the weather, keeping records of the wind direction and weather forecasts developed. School was taken as a centre, and four well-known landmarks were picked out to the north, south, east and west of it. This work developed into using an atlas to find the direction of north. The area around the school outside the children's everyday experience was discussed: mountains to the east, industry to the west, farmland to the south, and so on. Coach visits to these areas were arranged when children had check lists to fill in so that they could collect information. A talk on who might find the balloons led to group work on fishermen, hikers, shepherds, and farmers. Lots of simple arithmetical calculations were worked out, such as the cost of balloons for the class; the proportion of various colours, and so forth.

The second-year juniors concentrated on the historical aspects of ballooning and compiled an amazing history of ballooning from Da Vinci and the Montgolfiers to Zeppelins, barrage balloons, and weather balloons. Plotting replies gave impetus to the study of the areas from which balloons were returned.

The third-year juniors' really concentrated effort, by their own choice, turned out to be making some realistic models of the flying balloons of the eighteenth and nineteenth centuries, and writing some original poems about balloons. Individual studies were undertaken on dozens of topics suggested by the scheme and booklets were compiled.

In the top junior class, groups produced booklets of a high quality about the making of balloons, pure and synthetic rubber, the rubber-producing areas of the world, the science connected with using hydrogen to make the balloons rise, work on other gases and air, and a study of prevailing winds. Lots of arithmetic was tackled, bringing in speed, time, distance, scale drawing, costing, comparison of heights and distances travelled by balloon and car.

A large map was used in the hall to chart the replies we received. Lists of children and the number of their balloons were posted and a cross-reference list to chart the return of the tabs was also displayed.

Work was started on Monday and one balloon was released by each child on Friday of that week. Another batch of balloons was released the following Monday and replies from the Friday were by this time being received.

The venture was voted a huge success. We were all quite surprised at some of the facts that came out of this scheme. For example, one balloon had averaged about 40 m.p.h. on its 120 mile journey. Interest was renewed with every visit of the postman, especially when we had returns from such interesting places as the Jodrell Bank Telescope. It is hard to describe the excitement as the slips began to return—among the staff as well as the children—and for combining pleasure and purposeful learning the launching of these 'satellites', as the children called them, needed some beating.

An enterprise such as this strained the library resources of the school to the limit. There was a central library where about twelve children could work. It was comfortable, with good heating and carpet, but had been improvised from a disused entrance corridor. We also had classroom libraries in each class. Every class had a reference list of books available in the other classrooms and there were facilities for interchange. Cutforth and Battersby (1962), talking of whether to provide central library facilities conclude that, 'If a library is to add anything at all to the life of the school it must add something different to this' (classroom environment). I think our arrangements did just this. The central library provided a quiet room, the atmosphere of a library, always a display to provoke interest, comment, or a lead to sets of books. It provided a different kind of environment from the 'workshop' atmosphere of the classroom. In the classroom, on the other hand, were books needed for constant reference : children's encyclopedias, single reference texts, and special sets centred around work of the moment were withdrawn from the central or other class libraries. I concluded that when children were learning by discovery, both a class and a central library were needed in the primary school for efficient use of the total resources. After all, 'The value of the library depends as much on its power to provide a home for the intellectual life as upon the number of its books' (Mace, 1962).

From the description of this scheme I would like to pick out two classes for further comment as my personal observations, recorded at the time, are mainly concerned with these two groups.

The first was the first year junior group. As stated, the ideas for the scheme in this class came from the children. It was an interesting feature that they were particularly concerned with where the balloons would go immediately they were out of sight. They were now at the stage of wanting to know something outside their immediate environment. From this work, they wanted to find out what lay beyond the range of hills outside the village. They found out and several weeks later, went on a visit to see the mountains to the east, farmlands to the south, industry to the west, and fells to the north. This seems to me to be a method admirably suited to the developmental stage and needs of these children. The children were also interested in the people who might find the balloons. We were again lucky here as one balloon was returned from the radio telescope at Jodrell Bank and another was found by a titled lady in the grounds of her estate. Both these were followed up by letters and further interesting replies received. This is the stuff of real excitement to seven- and eight-year-olds. The joy and enthusiasm of these children at being associated with a scheme which brought such rewards was remarkable. A reporter came into school one day during this work. The children talked freely to him and of course, after he had gone, all wanted to be reporters (the basis for more work, not reported here). The reporter came to see me at 9.10 a.m. saying that he could only stay five minutes. I gave him a general picture of the scheme and two guides to show him around school. He left at 12.15 p.m. saying it was the most wonderful assignment he had undertaken in years. The class teacher was nearing retirement. She was a firm disciplinarian and ventured into this work with some reservation. Beneath her rather intractable aura, however, she had the real art of providing good starting points, insisting on sustained effort, and effectively rewarding any work of quality which was appropriate to a particular child.

The second scheme for more detailed comment is that of the third year junior class. Here the children chose to make models of flying balloons of the eighteenth and nineteenth centuries. This class had a teacher who was very interested in junk modelling. His enthusiasm spread to every group of children entrusted to him. It was no surprise to me when the work became basically modelling. The important point to notice here is how the work developed. The models were the starting point. They led the children to books for reference. The books showed the needs for plans, for measurement, for accuracy of representation (so important now to these nine- to ten-year-old children—unlike our first year class). All this subsidiary work was gathered together in booklet form and displayed with some poetry about balloons. Then their own poetry began to emerge. This was not of high quality as the class had not had very much experience of this type of work. Nevertheless, it was free, creative, and expressive, showing an interest in the scheme, ideas developing from it, and a child-like sense of involvement in the escapades of the early ballooners.

> Time to float, still and clean
> Time to think and steer
> Time to empty ballast sand
> Time to wonder how to land.
>
> Up and Up, up and up
> The balloon soars eagle high
> There's just a chance, a chance, a chance
> That heaven may be nigh.

This poem was easily the most lyrical and was influenced in structure by some poems the boy had read in the class-room; but behind the structure is his own sense of wonder and a role-playing insight into other people's lives, not uncommon in junior school children. Rather a coincidence that this boy's poem should include the element of time as the teacher notes in his records, 'The scheme was a valuable experience in ordering work from a starting point and in linking individual effort to the work of others. The work on early ballooners certainly gave the children a better feeling of historical time sense than I have noticed before.' (I think this happened because (a) the quality of the children's learning was high, (b) they had been involved in looking at the subject from so many different angles that a realization of where their own study fitted into the overall scheme was slowly beginning to come into focus.)

The bulb show—an all-school project

This scheme reveals the same pattern of work on indi-vidual, group, and class lines within the school framework.

The scheme is more confined by its very nature but does 'show clearly how strong and spontaneous an interest they do take in the things and events of the physical world' (Isaacs, 1930).

Most schools grow spring flowers from bulbs, but with varying degrees of enthusiasm, according to an ever-changing pattern of interest and ideas.

My staff and I began to wonder whether we were using our bulb growing to the best advantage in our school. We decided that as the idea of growing bulbs always appealed to the children, we would try to use a bulb show as a means of providing them with a series of real learning situations where the many small jobs involved were an essential part of making the show a success.

As the bulb show was to be the culminating point of all the work connected with the scheme, it was essential that careful planning should, as far as possible, ensure that this was a success. We sought the advice of a good wholesale dealer in bulbs. He told us which varieties we should use so that they would all flower roughly at the same time. He chose types of hyacinth, daffodil, and tulip.

There are, of course, many other kinds of spring flowers which can be grown. We found it advisable, however, to limit the types we grew, as the more varieties one handles, the more difficult it is to achieve a common flowering period.

The administration of the bulb show gave many opportunities for the children to help. A letter was drafted giving details of the scheme and prices were worked out from the wholesaler's lists. These prices were the basis for many meaningful problems involving comparison of prices.

We made an inclusive charge for bulbs, fibre, and a pot.

This was based on the basic cost to us plus 10 per cent which allowed us to buy prizes and extra bulbs for use in school. By contacting the makers, we bought a very adequate bowl for seven pence.

Incidentally, we then operated a scheme whereby children returned their pots just before we started on our bulb show work in autumn and we gave a credit note to be used against the inclusive charge for the next lot. Children who needed practice in practical arithmetic were responsible for these transactions.

Parents were asked to allow the children to fill in the order form and in school the children were responsible for dealing with the money, submitting accounts, editing the orders, filing them, and preparing a list of the numbers of each type of bulb we required from the dealer. When the bulbs arrived, the children distributed them, using the lists they had previously prepared.

A group of children worked out the amount of fibre we needed by weighing enough for one dozen bowls and then calculating the quantity required for larger numbers.

Each child potted his own bulbs in school and then took them home with instructions for their care. We tried to make sure that the bulbs were kept in similar conditions in individual homes as far as possible. Progress details were recorded and displayed in school, and diagrams were on view to show how the bulbs should look at a given date. Thus, it was possible to try to obtain a uniform flowering period.

Work was carried out in each class relating to the type of flowers we were growing and to the progress of our own particular flowers. Local horticultural shops were very helpful in providing pictures and information.

Ideas and work seemed to grow out of the topic according to the interests of the children and teachers. Oil paintings were a feature in one class, growing cactus plants followed in another, and making indoor gardens in a third.

In school, experiments with bulb growing were carried out. Bulbs that had been fed by different types of fertilizer and plant food were grown in the same conditions. The varying effects were noted and accounted for. We showed a film of the bulb fields in Holland and supplemented this with an eye-witness account of the same area.

Preparation for the bulb show was, of course, the most exciting part of the whole scheme for the children. They sent out invitations and asked a prominent local person to open the show and judge the exhibits. The local Parks Department was very helpful and provided a floral background display.

A committee of children was formed to organize the reception and display of the exhibits. Tickets were made out for every bowl, receipts given to competitors, and prizewinners' labels were produced.

One section was devoted to showing the work produced in connection with the show. Here, there was an array of art work, bowl-holders and decorated jackets for the earthenware pots, made in a variety of materials, and written work submitted by every class.

This consisted mostly of booklets on these topics: 'Growing our Bulbs', 'My Book of Spring Flowers', 'The Bulb Show', 'The History of the Tulip', 'The Dutch Bulb-Growing Industry', etc.

Various prizes were awarded at the show. The best bowl in the show, the best bowl in each class, and so on. We gave a prize for the bowl with the best potential, to encourage children whose flowers were late, and one or two prizes which depended on luck, so that everyone was encouraged to bring their exhibits even though they may not always have been first-class.

6

The development of a discovery learning situation and the need for records of progress

One of the criticisms sometimes made of informal learning is that either there is no apparent progression or it is not possible to show progression systematically. If there is a common feature running through the themes presented in this book it is surely that there is an element of progression in all the work. The natural, inquiring mind of young children, given freedom to explore, cannot stagnate but is forever on the look-out for new leads and interesting avenues to follow. In this situation it is essential that good records should be kept because it is through accurate recording that a picture of the child's progress is built up and that provision for further advancement is ensured. There are basically three types of record which can be kept in the primary school.

School records

These are usually the official record cards, issued by the local authority. They give all the details of the child's school career and family background and are comprehensive in this respect. They are cumulative and passed on from teacher to teacher, who report their various opinions as the child passes from class to class. They tend to be factual and indeed some contain objective assessments such as the results of standardized tests. These are, in fact, 'record cards' and I would distinguish them from 'record keeping'. The former merely record facts, results of objective or terminal tests, teacher's notes, and organizational details, while record keeping is concerned more with the child in the classroom taking part in many activities.

Teacher's records

These are records kept by the teacher who will have a variety of recording to do. His records may be of two types: (a) the recording of any objective tests, reading ages, skills, attainment and diagnostic tests, (b) the second aspect is by far the most important side of teacher recording. These are the notes and comments which the teacher makes day by day, minute by minute, often while the children he is observing are actually working. Some teachers will say that it is not possible, with large classes, to undertake recording of this kind. I am not suggesting that it is easy, indeed, I know it presents great difficulties, but it is vital and a way must be found to accomplish it. The teacher who makes a habit of recording observations quickly, in abbreviated form, while helping individuals or groups is usually well on the way to solving the problem. A handy note pad and pencil are essential. To sit down at the end of a day to try to make records is laborious and much less useful than recording as the class proceeds. As the emphasis in the classroom moves away from 'chalk and talk' and excessively detailed marking, this recording aspect of the teacher's work assumes more significance. The following list gives some ideas which may help teachers to keep useful records adapted to the particular work on hand.

Suggested outlines for recording discovery work with children

1 Details of the child: age, sex, approximate IQ, interests, problems, difficulties, or any other relevant information.

2 Description of the starting point of the study, the child's knowledge of the field, and possible areas of exploration at the teacher sees them. Show if the child's progress differed from your expectations—actual quotations showing creative or inventive thought are useful in evaluation.

3 Discussion of standards—how were these achieved? Did subsequent deep involvement create a desire for higher standards in the children?

4 Use of materials—what was provided? Did the children spontaneously add to it? Was there any evidence of unusual, creative, or inventive use of material?

5 Give examples of problem solving. Show how a child first recognized the problem and then solved it. Compare how you would have told the child to solve it in an authoritarian situation with how the child solved it using discovery methods.

6 Description of any creative writing, drawing, modelling, chart making etc. Trace from an informal handling or play situation to specific work on the theme.

7 Note any social consequences of the work. Comment on children of different ages working together and show the effect of this on them and the work.

8 Show how you added to the environment as the work progressed. Were there any effects of this addition? Show how you added booklets based on children's ideas.

9 Show how both you and the children used sources of information.

10 Show how the topic led to other fields—were any extensions suggested by the children?

11 Diagrammatic representation showing how your integrated study covered different areas of formal subjects.

12 Your personal conclusions.

By recording sections from this list, the teacher will be able to see how the children reacted to the present stimulus and established ideas for further progression. Social characteristics of the children will emerge, leaders and followers can be noted, as well as children showing withdrawal symptoms. Emotional problems will become evident and can be tackled; group as well as individual needs will become apparent.

Primary school children working on a scientific investigation are a good subject for this recording. It is here that we can see easily the progression of discovery learning. The development of lines of thought is clearly brought out by the physical nature of the experimental situation. Children arrange a set of circumstances and discuss the organization. They add, change, amend, delete, re-organize, and all the time are making decisions, giving reasons for the changes, and coming to terms with the views of others in the group. They then cause certain things to happen to their arrangement and watch these carefully, commenting on and assessing the changes taking place. After this comes the examination and evaluation of the results and more discussion. The teacher, listening, prompting, and recording the discussion through these stages can see the development of creative thinking and see possible lines for future development.

Some teachers will wish to record advances in skills as a priority and can devise a personal system for this. Others may find a task list useful to check off the progress of children from time to time. One such list used in an infant class covered these points:

1 Uses school library books well.
2 Understands library classification system.
3 Uses books for finding out.
4 Can tell a simple story.
5 Can read a story to a friend.
6 Knows address.
7 Can write address.
8 Can write own news.
9 Writes short stories.
10 Writes poetry.
11 Spells common words correctly.
12 Writes letters.
13 Takes care of property and materials.
14 Clears away spontaneously.
15 Can take a message.
16 Can accept a message and relay it accurately.
17 Organizes time efficiently.
18 Works conscientiously alone.
19 Works co-operatively with a group.
20 Knows the names of six other children outside his class.
21 Shows interest in neighbourhood environment.
22 Shows interest in classroom environment.
23 Brings to school things of interest.
24 Contributes to discussion.
25 Knows days of week.
26 Knows months of year.
27 Speaks clearly.

28 Plays games fairly.
29 Shows interest in discovery.
30 Uses spatial terms accurately.
31 Can tell the time.
32 Has made some models (a) independently (b) with a group.
33 Knows the seasons and seasonal activities.
34 Knows the highway code.
35 Can sing a song unaccompanied.
36 Can name three books on class bookshelf.
37 Can answer questions on these books.
38 Can play Kim's Game—20 objects—1 minute to view—how many were correctly remembered?
39 Knows the names of various meals.
40 Record any other noteworthy achievement.

This is a general list but teachers can apply the same principles in making more specific lists to check development of skills in reading and mathematical experiences.

At the nursery or reception stage, the teacher could look more specifically at play; recording groupings, direction, degree of imitation, imagination and co-operation shown and the types of play in which children were involved. Language is important here. The teacher can record extension of vocabulary and note the degree of comprehension and whether sentences were well formed and articulation good. A study of the child's questions could also give useful information. The teacher at this stage would be concerned particularly with emotional and social development, recording the child's degree of stability and examples of developing maturity.

Some teachers, especially in a vertically grouped class, find it useful occasionally to check the activities of each child in a class over a whole day. This requires additional help and can involve a nursery assistant, the head teacher, an aide or an auxiliary, but the advantages of seeing completely the pattern of children's activities from time to time are important.

You may be inclined to wonder, after thinking about the teacher as recorder, whenever the teacher has time to function as 'teacher'. Naturally, each teacher will resolve the demands of recording in a manner suitable to himself but it is important to realize that all teaching is weakened if it does not recognize the importance of the individual in a group situation, and recording is an aid to this end. In fact, the recording of a point is a way of clarifying it.

Pupil's records

This third kind of recording is particularly suitable to the junior school, although I know many infant classes where children keep their own records of their work. Just how detailed the records kept by the children will be depends on their age, training, and the type of classroom organization. Children need training in how to keep their own records, but they soon become adept. Below is a progress record one teacher used with an upper junior class. The children kept this for a month. It was useful as a record and as a stimulus to effort and quality. Children made additional entries from time to time especially when they had been involved in group schemes covering social studies themes, for which a provision was made on this form. This is a good example of the way in which the children will structure their own work, in this case improving on a provisional recording sheet as the teacher had drawn it up. The card used by the children was arranged in a folder containing enough room for a child's entries. Only the ideas for recording are given here.

My progress card

Name   Class

                    Month

Mathematics
Describe the experiments you did. Give an example of each type of calculation you used to solve the problem.
Note the page number and name of the book you used for further practice of these calculations.
Give the number of the test card used (if any).
Note any difficulty.
Have you noted this difficulty before?
Write down briefly what you did to help in any group work.

Reading
Books read.
Reasons for choosing each book.
Book review written?   Yes/No

Creative English
Give the titles of any written work and put a tick beside those that the teacher saw.

Spelling
New words.
Underline any new words which were not used in your own writing.

Science
Title of study.
Short summary.
Where is it recorded?
(individual or group book?)

Topic work
Give a short summary of:
1   Individual work,
2   Group work.
What have you enjoyed most this week?
What have you enjoyed least this week?
Special difficulties.
Anything else to record?

Hand this record to your class teacher at the end of each month. Remember, it should be initialled by the teacher each week.

I referred earlier to the difficulty of helping infant children to keep their own records. Inventive teachers, who believe in the value of self-kept records, will find ways of surmounting these difficulties. The system described below has worked successfully in both an infant and a slow learners' class. The teacher had prepared a booklet, one page of which is shown here, which was almost non-verbal so that the children had only to put ticks in the right spaces. The page shows only three activities. On subsequent pages, children added to the record if they had taken part in any of the following activities: shop, word games, sand play, weighing, reading, number games, using a stop-watch, clay, Wendy house. These occupations were all represented visually for easy identification. The list could be extended to cover the range of activities in any classroom. For example, in the slow learners' class, one section dealt with 'Things I can do' and children were able to record their practice and acquisition of such skills as tying knots, using scissors, swimming, riding a bicycle and a scooter.

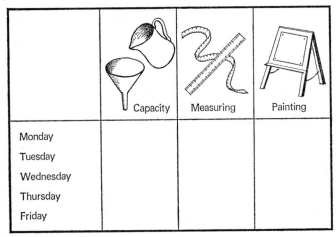

	Capacity	Measuring	Painting
Monday			
Tuesday			
Wednesday			
Thursday			
Friday			

Figure 1

Children can also record their own progress in other subjects: 'Things I can do in PE', 'Songs we know' or 'Our Prayers', or pinpoint 'My special difficulties'.

The teacher must be involved with the children's own records. Indeed, some teachers compile their own records from those kept by the children. Discussion of the pupil's own recordings with the teacher is an essential feature of this work. If the child of his own accord brings his record to the teacher to explain it and show the successes and problems he has had, there is a basis for partnership in solving the problems on hand. Children like to feel that they have been made responsible for part of their work and are trusted to report it accurately and participate in its evaluation. All this shows that the developing nature of discovery work is in some measure dependent upon an accurate system of observation and recording, carefully arranged and worked out for the needs of both the teachers and children who will be concerned with it, each one in his own way.

In a more detailed study of recording individual progress (Foster, 1971), I have extended many of the ideas introduced here. This work could be used as further reading on this topic for those who wish to study the subject in more depth.

7

Discovery learning—the question of organization

We may ask whether the accepted forms of organization are most suitable and effective for children learning by discovery methods. This is a basic question which teachers have been asking over the past decade and many recent changes in organization reflect the conclusions they have been reaching.

The internal organization of the school is quite rightly decided by the head teacher. Conditions vary so much from school to school that this arrangement is an essential feature of our educational system. In recent years, many head teachers have become dissatisfied with the grouping in their schools and a great deal of discussion and research has been concerned with whether some types of classification are more desirable than others. The focal points of discussion have been vertical grouping in the infants' school and streaming in the junior school.

Vertical grouping

Vertical grouping is generally thought of as a comparatively recent trend in infant schools. Indeed there has been a spread of this kind of organization over the last few years, but the idea was discussed many years ago. In 1933 a consultative committee published *The Nursery and Infants' Schools Report*. Referring to this type of classroom organization it said, 'On the other hand, many schools have experimented with what is known as a "vertical" classification. Here each class contains children of all ages from five to seven or eight, each occupied with work appropriate to his powers and they remain throughout the infant stage in the care of the same teacher.' This statement, written over thirty years ago, gives a perfect picture of vertical grouping as it is practised today, and much of the report is still surprisingly fresh and pertinent. My purpose here, therefore, to look at the trend and ascertain whether it is in keeping with established principles of growth and development at the infant school stage, is straightforward.

Vertical grouping attempts to assimilate children into school in an easy manner, avoiding some of the more obvious traumatic experiences usually associated with many new children coming together at the same time, in the same class. It is also claimed that a better child/teacher relationship is built up over the longer period of time. These two claims are associated, the teacher acquires a more intimate knowledge, and older children help the younger ones to adjust to the school situation. The older children are said, in their turn, to benefit from the position of trust they take up. The able help the less able and the classroom is more like the natural setting of a large family. Blyth (1965) calls this form of grouping 'a more effective method', when comparing various forms of infant school organization, but he does point out that a feature of the system is the necessity for the entire school or at least the lower part of it to be organized on these lines. It is perhaps useful to point out here that very many of our primary schools are vertically grouped by necessity. Almost 50 per cent of our primary schools have under 100 children on the roll and adopt mixed-age grouping as a matter of course.

Ridgway and Lawton (1965) give a good descriptive account of vertical grouping in action and show how this form of arrangement does in fact cater efficiently for children in the unstructured atmosphere of the modern infant school.

There are many advantages claimed for vertical grouping and most teachers sympathize with the aims of the scheme. There are, however, a great many practical difficulties calling for special gifts on the part of the teacher which most teachers would like to see carefully studied under controlled conditions before embarking on the change-over to a vertical classification. Mycock (1966) has carried out an investigation, as yet unpublished, which compares children in a good horizontally grouped situation with similar children who are vertically grouped. The tentative findings in this particular scientifically controlled piece of research are that vertical grouping did facilitate adjustment to school in the initial stages to a greater extent than a horizontal arrangement. The writer also noted the advantages of an increased social interaction and lengthened pupil/teacher relationships in the vertically grouped classes.

It seems that here is a trend which appears to be linked up with conditions emphasizing the importance of learning through experience and discovery. There are many problems still to be faced regarding classroom organization at the infant level, but vertical groupings must be examined as a possibility. But one thing must be emphasized: it would be quite wrong to change from any form of rigid organization, if in fact any still exists in infant schools, to a form of vertical grouping simply as part of a trend. Vertical grouping, with the flexible, informal structures inherent in its organization, must be the natural progression from the informal activities of a relatively tolerant setting in a horizontally grouped class. It is only when children are already learning individually at their own rate, in a natural setting, that vertical grouping can be introduced with a reasonable hope of success.

Streaming/non-streaming

Until about a decade ago, the most usual way to group children in the junior school was to divide them into 'streams' according to some assessment of their academic ability. This presupposes, of course, that in the school there were enough children to make more than one class for each year. This streaming was principally the result of the views relating to the nature of intelligence held during the 1930s. (See Hadow, 1931.) It was also a measure of expediency in arranging for the selection of children for a particular type of secondary school at 11-plus. The consultative committee's report on the primary school (Hadow, 1931) recommended a wider, more active approach to the education of young children and also at the same time proposed that children should be classified according to 'their natural gifts and abilities', suggesting that wherever possible a streamed organization should be instituted: 'A series of "A" classes for the bright children, and a series of smaller "C" classes or groups to include retarded children, both series being parallel to the ordinary series of "B" classes or groups for the average children.'

In the early 1950s the practice of streaming came under criticism on the grounds that the very process of dividing children into streams as the result of some very highly suspect assessment of their ability ensured that differences between children on entry to school became accentuated. Since then, a great deal of work has been carried out into the merits and de-merits, advantages and disadvantages of streaming as a form of grouping. The interested reader can read some of this evidence in more detail in these publications:

Bouri, J. and Barker Lunn, J. C. (1969) *Too small to stream. A study of grouping in small junior schools*, National Foundation for Educational Research.

Barker Lunn, J. C. (1970) *Streaming in the primary school*, National Foundation for Educational Research.

Daniels, J. C. (1961) 'The effects of streaming in the primary school', *British Journal of Educational Psychology*, February and June 1961.

Jackson, B. (1964) *Streaming: an educational system in miniature*, Routledge & Kegan Paul.

Willig, C. J. (1963) 'Social implications of streaming in the junior school', *Educational Research*, No. 2, Vol. 5.

To sum up the findings indicated in these studies, it would seem that there is some evidence accumulating that there are many advantages associated with the non-streamed class, and some points of concern to be noted regarding the practice of streaming.

Some teachers still make out a case for streaming, saying that it is the only arrangement which extends the most able pupils and encourages the weakest. They contend that the demands of the 11-plus necessitate this form of grouping and that results show that the practice has been successful. They suggest that less able children feel inferior when placed with children of a higher academic ability and that there are facilities for easy transfer if necessary between the streams. The books listed on page 88 suggest answers to most of these arguments. For example, it is shown that to be effective, transfer would need to involve about 20 per cent of the children whereas in actual practice, the transfer rate is often less than 5 per cent.

A strong case has been built up to show that streaming is not wholly desirable as a system of grouping. It has been shown that streaming tends to reflect social class much more than real ability. Children in unstreamed classes are shown to have higher levels of social adjustment in some cases, and to be working in a more effective educational environment. Streaming can also have an adverse effect on younger children within a twelve month age range, i.e., those children whose birthdays fall in the spring or early summer. The differences in academic attainment between children taught in streamed and unstreamed classes is not clearly defined, and neither grouping can be shown to provide a clear-cut advantage over the other in this respect but teachers in unstreamed classes seem to be catering better for children's learning on a more individual basis.

From my own experience of working in streamed and unstreamed classes, I believe that if one wishes to arrange for children to learn by discovery methods, an unstreamed organization seems preferable. I do feel though that to change from streamed to unstreamed classes merely to conform with a trend is to exchange a system having some merits for one which may be less effective. A change of this kind must come about as part of a fundamental re-thinking of methods, aims, purposes, and techniques in the classroom. If the same formal methods are used with an unstreamed class as were practised with a streamed one, the results will be less successful. The process of de-streaming has to be accompanied by a change to discovery methods, allowing the children to take part in their own research schemes and to participate, through practical experience, in the work on hand.

It is where children are given a wide range of opportunity, in an atmosphere which encourages free interchange of ideas, that they are likely to find an activity in which they are successful. A premium must not be put on formal academic learning. Other attributes, skills, and interests must also be recognized as being socially valuable and encouraged, rewarded, and praised. In this way children of less than average academic ability may experience the successes sometimes confined to children with high verbal reasoning ability. In this way, their self-concepts are improved and with this new realization of success, they can tackle their skills, learning with new fervour, and often showing enhanced ability. This kind of practice is more likely to occur in an unstreamed class where both good standards of work and social interaction are apparent. Here the less able children have the spur of quality close at hand and at the same time are given an opportunity to experience this sort of success in a sphere where they are able to achieve it. This stimulus is seldom found in 'B' and 'C' classes where the sense of failure sometimes seems bred into the general atmosphere.

I have described many kinds of grouping in earlier chapters—but a general feature of all the groups was the fact that they were unstreamed. It seems impossible to lay down hard and fast rules about the advantages and disadvantages of the various groupings. What seems to be required is a system in which each child has the freedom to decide whether he works on individual or group lines. From our experience, in the social milieu of the classroom children will change easily from individual to group work and vice versa. The children themselves are probably the best judge of what they need at any particular time and I have no evidence that in the right sort of atmosphere this interchange will not take place. The class and all-school project seemed to be valuable as re-vitalizers—their novelty value must not be underestimated. A student recently reported: 'The children enjoyed the parts I would have found tedious, largely, I suspect, because of the novelty.' It is the initial surge the projects give to children which is important. The individual and group work begins to develop and range outwards from the initial concept after the children have become interested.

The less able children seem to follow a fairly well-defined pattern in this work. They prefer a cosy, group situation at first where their confidence can be built up and where they can ask before each stage so that they avoid making mistakes which might make them look foolish. Once they have found their feet and gained confidence, they like to branch out into a piece of individual work. This usually takes the form of a booklet, most of which is likely to be copied from textbooks. This is a stage which needs careful handling by the teacher. It must be accepted and appreciated. It must also be seen as a transition stage and a child led from this stage to producing creative, free written work where he gives information and individual comment in his own words. When the less able child reaches this stage, a tremendous improvement in standards may confidently be looked for. What is more important, an improvement may be anticipated in the child's general approach to school, his friends, and himself, because now he regards himself as a successful person, one who respects and is respected.

School organization involves both curriculum and syllabus as these again are the province of the head teacher. The studies reported here give abundant evidence that young children are not bound by conventional subject barriers if they are actively involved in their own learning. Neither will they be bound by the rigid dictates of a formal timetable. Most teachers have long ago realized this and plan the programme on broad integrated lines with the most flexible timetable arrangements. Yet there are still many primary schools where subjects appear on a rigidly enforced timetable, frustrating the spirit of inquiry which abounds in most schools. A measure of specialization in these schools requires a fixed timetable. One teacher recently showed me evidence that only on one day a week was it possible for his class to work for more than one hour without being taken away from its task to fit in with the dictates of the timetable. This is most frustrating to both teacher and children who want to continue working on interesting themes and yet are constantly prevented from doing so. The same teacher also reports frustration on the part of the specialist teacher coming in to take geography while the class teacher goes to another class to take games. The geography becomes another fragmented, compartmentalized unit, unconnected for the children with that which they consider their real work and thus unsatisfactory for the visiting teacher. Why do some schools still persist in dividing the class, boys to craft and girls to needlework? Both these skills should be acquired certainly, but as an integrated part of the work of the class. The dreary, intricate needlework, a relic of the Victorian era, which girls in the primary school sometimes do is undesirable. The work must be bold, free, imaginative, and with wider connections associated with their other inquiries. In this situation, boys are ardent needleworkers for short spells. They will work hard on their collage, to complete it as a background for their models. Quite rightly, they have no long term interest or finesse, they treat it as their work in just another aspect of craft. On the other side, how often I have heard girls complain that 'we never do any craft'.

As the timetable and the division of work into subjects exerts a stifling influence on the work of young children so does the formal syllabus. Luckily, schools generally are not bound by a syllabus to be 'covered' during the year. In some schools, the syllabus still exists in the teacher's drawer but is never used. The work illustrated in this book was born out of complete freedom from a syllabus. It is not possible to decide beforehand (in some cases four years beforehand) what children's interests will be at a particular time. The work must emerge from a declared interest, a question, or a request for information. It may come from a stimulus the teacher gives but it cannot emerge spontaneously from a previously ordered area of work. My syllabus would be 'that which has been accomplished at the end of the session'.

In my experience, teachers prefer the school scheme to explain general aims and an underlying philosophy of the work they are undertaking. The scheme which is appreciated is the one which gives guidance on *how* the work shall be organized rather than *what* shall be done. It may be necessary and even desirable to have a continuous 'skills record' outlined and recorded on a cumulative basis.

Some teachers like the thread of a reading scheme to run through an infant school but this must never be a whole pattern; it must be the skeleton which is clothed with a variety of other reading and writing experiences. If a pattern is considered necessary in any part of the curriculum, it must be such that it both accepts other interests and provides starting points for children's natural learning.

The reading scheme is successfully integrated into some of the most progressive infant school work. Where this happens, the scheme is used when interest in a subject is high. It is used as a means of helping a child to acquire a skill which he can use practically, to follow up and extend an interest. A child of five, six, or seven years does not suffer delays gladly. A skill has to be used, to personal advantage, quickly. The practice provided by a reading scheme is undertaken willingly if it is allied with the use of reading books selected by the child for a compelling reason. I would explain carefully to a child how the reading scheme works and the way in which it is built up to help him read more easily. The scheme must live, have purpose, and be accepted by a child if it is to be useful. At its best, it will be used with joy, while at its worst, it will lower and limit a child's interest, reduce his desire to develop his ability, and become progressively more sterile. In order to use a reading scheme in this flexible way, the class organization must be geared to the individual acquisition of skills and progress must be recorded in a personal way. In an activity like reading, where progress will vary so much from child to child, a class or sometimes even a group approach can have little validity.

Team teaching

The two main aspects of organization discussed, vertical grouping and streaming, have far-reaching implications on the planning of discovery learning. There is another movement, albeit still in its infancy in British primary schools, which needs to be considered in this context. This is team teaching. There are some isolated experiments being carried out but there has not been the scientific approach of setting up a well-documented experimental situation in England as there has been in America to evaluate the system. Team teaching, as it comes to us from America, means that instead of teachers working on their own, teams are organized and units of work are planned so that experienced and able teachers assume more responsibility, new teachers are gradually integrated into the system, and non-teaching staff are used under supervision. A team of teachers may be responsible for the work of 150 children, and teaching groups may vary from five to 150 according to the nature of the activity. For example, five pupils may work with one teacher to plan an intricate model while 150 children may all gather together to watch a film or receive instructions. Under this system pupils usually have a base room and a teacher who has special responsibility for their particular welfare.

In Great Britain many good primary schools are evolving a system of team teaching in the course of their normal work without attempting it on an organized or highly structured basis.

Forward-looking teachers are beginning to look again at the traditional one teacher, one classroom, thirty-five to forty-five children organization. The idea of the teacher as the focal point of the classroom has been losing ground; learners and learning replacing the teacher. Also the idea of the self-contained classroom is seen less and less in primary schools. Children are spilling out into corridors, the entrance hall or an annexe, carrying on a multitude of finding-out activities. It is from these situations that an informal type of team teaching is emerging in primary schools. As formal barriers and traditional views are broken down, as classroom doors are opened to allow free traffic, so children begin to approach other teachers than their own for help. One teacher, being an acknowledged source of help for modelling, is sought after, while another, perhaps in charge of the library, is seen as the person to approach for help in finding suitable books. This is a natural progression for the school moving to a more informal approach. A school organized on traditional lines trying to move to this system overnight would be faced by chaos. It is only by moving gradually, over a period of time, that children accept this way of working. I have seen schools move from a streamed to an unstreamed organization. This brought a change from formal to informal methods, changing the emphasis from class to groups and individuals. The next step was the informal use of teachers for special help, and it was at this stage that more detailed thought was given to organization and some experiments in team teaching were tried out. It is my opinion that for team teaching to be worth while in the primary school and to be compatible with discovery learning techniques, this is one of the patterns which its development and extension might take. There may be others evolved by schools which are suitable for them in their particular situation. The progressions outlined have been seen to work and have evolved naturally, the impetus for them coming from the children, surely one sign that this is a type of planning we must examine at this time.

Team teaching is defined by Shaplin and Olds (1964) as 'A type of instructional organisation, involving teaching personnel and the students assigned to them in which two or more teachers are given responsibility for working together, for all or a significant part of the instruction of the same group of students.' (This book also gives a full theoretical basis of the system.) The suggested aim is to improve instruction and promote greater personal growth. Any form of team teaching at the primary level must stress integration, activity, intrinsic motivation, and participation. Children must still continue to learn through practical experience and by discovery principles. It may be that a team teaching programme, and some schemes outlined in this book would fall into this category, could be specifically organized once or twice each term. A topic might be taken, discussed, and prepared by the team of teachers and worked out subsequently with a group of children, the theme culminating in a display of the work produced. The display would be a co-ordinating factor so that all the children would see the unity of the whole scheme. The themes for this type of work would probably be wide, leaving room for flexibility of thought and change in emphasis as children worked productively on the material. Peoples of the world, shelter, food, clothes, could all be used as broad starting points which could develop along lines suitable for the particular children.

It is in a team teaching situation that auxiliaries could play a purposeful role in the education of young children. Pedan (1964), in an article 'A new pattern for the primary school' in *The Head Teacher's Review* reports the work of helpers in this situation in America.

> In order to free the teaching staff for this [analysing and planning the work] and to allow more time for teaching, each team has a clerical assistant who undertakes every kind of secretarial service for the team. This includes typing and duplicating, ordering supplies, making inventories, filing records, organising materials for class lessons, maintaining class registers and attendance sheets, and correcting tests where no evaluation is required. Some schools provide a second helper for each team whose duties include supervising pupils in the playground, dining hall and cloakroom, assembling and organising audio-visual apparatus, and assisting teachers in the care of the classroom—watering plants, arranging furniture, setting up wall displays and bulletin boards. In short the clerical and teacher aides do the hundred and one non-teaching tasks which have always been included in the duties of the teachers.

In this system, aides can be efficiently used in well-defined non-teaching areas of the work, under the guidance of qualified staff, freeing teachers to do the professional work for which they are trained.

Team teaching may be one way to supervise effectively the very flexible groupings which can be produced in a developing discovery learning situation. Independent study, small group instruction for particular skills, large group instruction for films, introductory lessons, and testing diverse groupings can all be organized as part of a plan, where progressional skills can be catered for, recorded, and evaluated.

There are many aspects of team teaching that teachers will wish to consider before embarking on this kind of organization. It has been my intention here to show that it can be reconciled with progressive education. Many teachers, in examining their work, will see the areas where they can truly say they already approach a form of team teaching. It is in the refinement and consequent re-thinking of this aspect of their work that schools will evolve the right approach to this technique for their own schools, and perhaps cater more effectively in providing challenging learning situations for their pupils.

Whatever organization is tried within the school, it must be remembered that it must cater for teachers and pupils, both having their own needs and problems. To those responsible for school planning I would quote from Spencer (1963) that, 'A good system is twice blessed—it blesses him that trains and him that's trained.' The interested reader would find the work of Freeman (1969) and Warwick (1971) useful as follow-up reading on this topic.

Organization—some practical issues

While my remarks on the advantages of a more informal, discretional approach are made with complete sincerity, my experience as a headmaster and college of education lecturer has made me realize that the ideal in teaching style is not reached without considerable professional toil. Indeed, 'the ideal teaching style' will vary from person to person. The injunction, 'Go and watch Mrs Smith and see how she does it', commonly referred to in some jobs as learning by 'sitting next to Nellie', has very little value to the average probationer teacher. What is needed is for the inexperienced teacher to work alongside a more seasoned colleague, become acquainted with the basis of the organization and the methods for implementing it, and see the complexities of the pupil/teacher interaction and relationship. Then the teacher must personalize this experience, and assimilate what is most appropriate to the successful parts of his own teaching style. In this way, he broadens his own approach by extending his work in that area where he feels most secure. Progress will be slow for many people, and many educational props may be required. It is easy, for example, for the successful, experienced infants' headmistress to assert, 'there is no need for a formal reading scheme'. This may be very true for her. It is a risky generalization to assume that all her staff can work efficiently without an ordered scheme, or in fact that they wish to do so. We pay a great deal of attention to the individuality of the child, less to individual differences in teachers.

Teachers with limited experience and expertise in organizing flexible individual and group activities can easily lose track of classroom activities, and their usefulness is then soon eroded. In this situation, I have advocated for some time now the use of a 'second system organization'. By this I mean that there should be a series of purposeful activities, readily available, which can be used by children if they cannot carry on with their immediate activities because the teacher is just not available for consultation. These second system activities are not merely to keep children occupied, nor do they perform a purely therapeutic function. They should have a definite aim, and should generally be concerned with using a skill which has been recently acquired. In a class of nine-year-olds, the whole class had been engaged in activities centred round the title. 'Printing without a press'. They had been introduced to a variety of printing devices, and had collected a variety of articles which printed effectively. The classroom was organized with a work bay for creative crafts, and one day I noticed two boys working on this activity while they were waiting for the teacher to help them organize the information they had been gathering on carbo- hydrates. When the teacher was ready, they took their material, put it in their own open shelf and carried on with her. Two essentials emerge. First, the activity was available to the boys, and secondly, they put it away when they were able to resume their work on carbohydrates. The downfall of many permissive organizations is gross untidiness, inefficient filing, and badly-used storage.

In active learning classrooms, a routine must be estab- lished. Rules must be few and simple, they must be under- stood by the class, but they must be obeyed. Apparatus and equipment must be available but it must be self- checking so that it is returned after use. Above all, material of all descriptions must be available on a self-help basis. Training is needed here so that the class know what is acceptable usage and conduct. The norm of the classroom is quickly established both with regards to behaviour, and use of stock, but it remains to be emphasized that initially, there has been some direction before responsible habits have been built up. Too often, student teachers only see the end result, and presume it was always like that. What they have missed in most cases is the teacher's spade-work when attitudes were formed, and acceptable patterns of behaviour were delineated.

I have discussed some of the principles behind the organization of an informal learning classroom and shown the practical difficulties of implementing them. I do not believe there is any one system of organization which will ensure success, but that an individual teacher will achieve a greater measure of quality in her work if she plans meticulously, hastens slowly, leads from her strength, and makes a conscious effort to evaluate her work and involve the children in this assessment. Where children are being asked to assume a measure of responsibility for their conduct, they must be helped to attain this by going through a stage where responsibility is shared. I saw this well illustrated by a gifted student who, faced with a very noisy class, helped them, over a period of a fortnight, first to become aware of the noise; secondly, to see that it was an inhibiting factor, and thirdly to try to reduce it. Gradually, from 'nagging' the children about the noise, she helped them to assume responsibility for its curtailment. So ultimately, most classrooms and work areas will evolve on individual lines. This is essential. It used to be thought in colleges of education that demonstration classrooms showed students exactly how to arrange their own classrooms in school. Nothing could be more rigid than a replication of one theoretically good design. A pattern, conceived in isolation, without thinking of the needs of a particular group of children, the personalities of the teachers, and the peculiarities of the building is not the best model to copy. Rather, what is needed is an understanding of the principles involved in the method, a knowledge of the pitfalls, a sense of timing, a flexibility of approach, a willingness to retrieve failure, and a desire to adventure sensibly. With these guidelines, I believe any teacher can provide the positive setting which is needed in primary schools today.

The organization of a discovery learning classroom—how to begin—a case study

I have already shown that there is rarely 'a royal road'

to success, or a 'black-box' system which can be successfully applied by everyone concerned with planning children's discovery learning. The previous section outlined
some of the principles which govern practical decisions
which teachers must take, and gave indications of some
of the possible stages and procedures which a successful
teacher must consider. The aim of this section is to give
a résumé of the steps taken by one teacher beginning to
work on less formal lines. Details of her class programmes
for one term will be given, and supported by a commen-
tary on the difficulties she encountered and how these
were resolved. In this way, it is hoped that students,
and teachers who are inexperienced in this way of working, will be able to apply some of the ideas given in the
book, to their own situations, and analyse more clearly
their own teaching styles and their didactic roles.

THE TEACHER Mrs A. was thirty-five years old when
she qualified as a mature student. The work described was
undertaken during the third term of her first year.

THE SCHOOL The school was built in 1936 and had
begun life as a secondary school. Recently it had become
a primary school but no extensive alterations had been
carried out to equip the building for its new purpose. It
was built on the 'double quadrangle-surrounding class-
room-central hall' principle popular at that time. The
head was very experienced and anxious to encourage
innovation. He gave full support to Mrs A.'s ideas and
helped her in every way. The classroom was large, had
running water, and access to a corridor which served as
additional working space.

THE CLASS There were thirty-seven boys and girls aged
nine and ten years. They were a mixed-ability group and
came from a wide range of social class backgrounds.

Attainment was generally good, and only three children had reading ages of less than eight years. There was a high proportion of broken homes represented in the class considering that there seemed to be little shortage of material possessions. Parental interest was high. There was a boisterous element in the class which had caused Mrs A. some concern during the first two terms of her appointment.

PREAMBLE TO THE WORK IN QUESTION Teachers in the school generally had a free hand with class activities and organization. There was little central direction. This led to a diversity of practice and standards. Inexperienced teachers would have preferred more direct guidance on curriculum content, planning and evaluation.

Mrs A. had been left to find her own feet, and during the first term she reported that she, 'attempted too much too soon'. Apparently she had tried to implement a full, integrated programme with a large element of free choice. This had led to frustration and a general dissatisfaction with the work. From this background, she had sought advice and from this, a more specific programme emerged for the third term.

THE AIM OF THE PROGRAMME The aim of this programme was to present a basic organization from which children could adventure freely, on active discovery lines. It was felt essential to provide experiences on individual, small group, and class bases. Also, the teacher wished to have close contact with activities so that some objective evaluation of the scheme could be carried out, and also to try to ensure that the approaches used were viable and economical. With this pattern, it was hoped to check some of the unruliness which had been apparent previously, and to raise standards generally.

THE ORGANIZATION OF THE PROGRAMME On the advice

of the head teacher, Mrs A. planned her work in these broad areas: the acquisition of mathematical and language skills, topic work covering the creative activities/humanities, physical education, religious education, and musical experiences.

THE ACQUISITION OF MATHEMATICAL SKILLS There was a supply of books from the series *Let's Explore Mathematics*, Marsh L. G. (A. & C. Black) in the class, and Mrs A. decided to use these, together with a variety of other mathematics work-books which were available. These books were used in conjunction with an assignment-card system. Often the sequence was as follows:

1 A group were involved in practical work and recording of findings.

2 The teacher ascertained the type of calculation which had been encountered, often gave specific help with this and introduced related computational ideas in a teaching situation.

3 Assignment cards, involving these calculations, and further practice of the skills were given out. These cards generally provided a reference to the textbooks already mentioned.

The chart, *Guidelines in School Mathematics*, produced by the Mathematics Department of the Manchester College of Education (Rupert Hart-Davis) was used to outline the mathematical concepts appropriate to this group so that a full range of mathematical ideas was covered during the course of the term. Using this method, individual work developed from practical experience in groups, and on occasions, the class was drawn together when a general teaching point occurred. About one hour each day was devoted to this work.

THE ACQUISITION OF LANGUAGE SKILLS During the term,

special emphasis had been given, at some time, to these areas: reading, personal writing, speech and drama, comprehension, recording data, sentence patterning, calligraphy, poetry, literature, and spelling.

Often, language activities linked directly with work in the creative activities/humanities (examples of this are given subsequently). Usually, activities arose out of interest shown through questions, discussion, investigation in the library, ideas generated by the interest table, etc. These were frequently taken up spontaneously and developed. All activities were noted carefully, however, and any undue balance cautiously corrected in time. Sometimes, Mrs A felt the need for specific work. These needs often showed themselves in written work, or when queries arose. In this case, special programmes were followed for as long as seemed appropriate. An example of this can be given. Many of these children were capable of a high standard of written expression. Mrs A. became dissatisfied with the poor quality of sentence construction being offered. Specific help was given here consisting of: (a) direct teaching, (b) finding examples of different sentence structures in books, (c) exercises, (d) personal writing specially geared to this particular aspect. In this way, Mrs A. identified a need and catered for it specifically, but retained an element of personal activity and finding-out in her programme.

In summary, the language experiences were a blend of freedom to follow personal interests and extend them, and organized, prepared, contrived material often in line with the declared interests. The time spent on these activities was about one and a half hours daily.

TOPIC WORK COVERING THE CREATIVE ACTIVITIES/HUMANITIES Creative activities/humanities is used here to describe the range of activities which cover two and three dimensional arts and crafts. These creative activities are usually allied to a topic from one of the humanities. Thus, topic work, themes, projects, research work and the like are all included under this heading.

During the term, Mrs A.'s class were concerned with two major themes, each basically occupying half a term. The first half-term was concerned with a study of 'Texture', an interest in which had been shown during the previous term. This interest had been noted but not followed up at that time.

The teacher arranged the initial stimulus in much the same way as in many of the schemes reported earlier. She drew heavily on Card 6, Set 2 of *To Point the Way* (Foster and Selby, 1966) (see page 28), in arranging these experiences.

On the interest table, she placed examples of lace, rubber, brick, wool, fur, a washer, pumice stone, polythene, corrugated paper, cork, loofah, shells, nuts, twigs, bark, coal, coke, pottery, iron, steel and cloth. Suggestions were made for categorizing them, and games described to use them. For example, guessing the names of objects by touch only while blindfold, and floatation experiments. Unusual uses were asked for, different combinations to produce something new, and suggestions for collage.

Most of these suggestions were taken up. Many involved written work, and mathematical measurement and calculation. Work was collected in large work-books where many children contributed on occasions. At other times, individual books were made. An interest developed in mosaics. Broken pottery was collected and mosaics were built up in trays containing plaster of paris, Polyfilla, cement, and glues. A history of mosaics was studied. Visits were made to see good examples of this art, and books were produced on Greek and Roman mosaics.

The second half-term, the theme was concerned with 'Shadows and reflections'. This was organized on similar lines to the texture work but Mrs A. found that in requisitioning material for this type of work, her basic needs were for plentiful supplies of paper, paint, and such items as scissors, Sellotape, staplers etc., and less for exercise books. Also textbooks were less important than easy-to-use reference books on related topics.

Shadows and reflections began with a display on the interest table. This included torches, articles chosen for their unusual shapes, mirrors, prisms, lenses, a magic lantern, and pictures showing reflections and shadows. Several passages from books and poems on the subject were also available. Suggestions for initial exploration were given and all the class had a silhouette of their profile taken. These were then used in a 'guess the profile' session.

The early experiments with shapes, lighting and reflection led to mathematical work on symmetry, tessellations and area. English work produced descriptive passages, poems and recording of scientific data. Art work was varied; particularly fine techniques were developed, through direct teaching, to show how to indicate reflections. Models to achieve interesting shadows developed without any help or guidance. The time spent on this work was between 1½ and 2 hours per day.

PHYSICAL EDUCATION This was organized along lines followed in school. A full description of this is outside the scope of this résumé but the work formed an entity in itself containing elements of movement, educational gymnastics, games skills and swimming.

RELIGIOUS EDUCATION This was organized in line with

the agreed syllabus used by the local education authority. Mrs A. placed an emphasis on practical work and most discussions of moral and ethical values grew either from personal relationships in the class, or in discussion of paintings and models concerned with biblical stories.

MUSICAL EXPERIENCES Music was taken by a specialist. During this time Mrs A. either prepared material for her own class or helped with a remedial organization which existed in the school.

SOME COMMENTS ON THE SCHEME

1 The greater element of organization, and the more efficient detailing of 'who did what' in the classroom paid dividends to this teacher in her probationary year.

2 Planning was a significant factor in the success of the scheme.

3 Changes were made gradually. The initial organization was kept as a basis and innovation was carried out cautiously.

4 Particular attention was paid to the groups in which the children would work. These were carefully planned in consultation with the class. They were acceptable and harmonious units.

5 Writing down a statement of objectives was valuable.

6 Listing provisions to be made was also useful.

7 It was essential to provide activities for slow learners and gifted children.

8 Appeal needed to be made to all the senses. It was tempting to appeal to the visual sense and neglect the others at times.

9 A record of progress in basic skills was essential.

10 Reference material needed to be detailed carefully before a topic began.

11   Consultation with the head teacher was particularly useful at all stages.

12   A plan of the classroom arrangements (wallboards, tables, window ledge displays, special corners, dividers, book units etc.) and how these might change was desirable.

13   A notebook was essential in which significant happenings concerning both groups and individuals was recorded. From this notebook, ideas for subsequent work often emanated.

14   Mrs A. made specific reference in her notes to her role as observer. The need to stand back and take a detached view of activities was essential. Inexperienced teachers are sometimes too submerged in the activities and fail to comprehend the total picture.

15   The main aim was to work to achieve a relaxed style of teaching. This was not easy but seemed to be essential for success.

8

Discovery methods and the slow-learning child

According to Bruner (1961), the highest state of human autonomy and perfection is reached when the individual discovers for himself relationships in his social and physical environment. An essential feature of Bruner's hypothesis is the seeing of relationships. We know that this is one of the real problems of slow learners; that they have more difficulty than abler children in perceiving relationships. We may, therefore, ask about the relevance of discovery methods for slow learners. In my experience, gained from the analysis of the material evaluated in this book, it would appear that, providing certain safeguards are taken, discovery methods can be used to real effect with slow-learning children.

Most teachers are familiar with the situation where they have set slow-learning children a 'finding-out' task and realized very quickly that these same children were all too easily distracted and led off into other activities, often of an anti-social kind. It is essential to control the stimuli presented to slow learners. An over-stimulating environment offers too much in the way of alternatives.

There is, in this situation, a need to limit the possibilities of choice of items necessary for discovery to be made. Alan, Tom and Mark had very poor academic attainment levels. All had IQs of between eighty and ninety and were usually in the forefront of any misbehaviour in the class. The teacher, in her first teaching year, set them the task of taking the lighting arrangements from a doll's house and using it in a lighthouse and boat shed which had been built previously. At first they were given no guidance. She reports a great deal of argument and confusion. Their approach was unorganized and haphazard. After a time they drifted away and began other activities of a routine nature, e.g., pressing nails into a block of clay, which seemed to satisfy them. The teacher called them together and showed them a single circuit set up on a board which was part of a science table display. They were soon able to see how to make the bulb work in this arrangement and educed the principle of completing the circuit. 'Can you find any similar circuits in the doll's house lights?' asked the teacher.

'It would be better if we took the wiring out.' (They did this.)

'What do we do with it now?'

'Would taking it to pieces help?' (Teacher.)

'We could wire it up like the other one (the other circuit) if we use one bulb and one wire.'

So the discussion carried on. What had happened was that the teacher had given the children fewer possibilities of choice. In this case they were able to see the relationships necessary to work the simple circuit and enjoyed completing this. As they took the other wiring to pieces, they discovered that in fact three circuits similar to the one brought by the teacher were involved in the doll's house lighting. These three lighting arrangements had simply been wired to the same battery. They assembled these quickly on the table and the teacher noticed how co-operation increased at this point. As soon as they felt as though they were succeeding, they began to work together more harmoniously. After seeing how the circuits worked, they put the lighting into the lighthouse and boat shed with ease. These three boys had achieved a great deal using a discovery approach, but there had been selection exercised by the teacher. She had organized the discovery so that the steps were seen more clearly but the boys, for their part, had formulated hypotheses and tested them ('See if that battery will light two lots of lights'), discounted unrelated alternatives, and redefined the problem in a more meaningful way.

Motivation plays a most important part in any attempt to use discovery methods with less able children. They need more encouragement and more praise from the teacher ('You are doing really well now, I am pleased') in order to become intrinsically interested rather than led on by the external incentives of such things as stars and 'house' points. It is when this motivation from within is achieved that these children develop a better image of self-capability and approach new problems with the feeling that as individuals they can accomplish something worthwhile.

The less able child has usually had to endure considerable failure. In these circumstances, he quickly develops an attitude of 'I don't understand', without really making any effort. It is easier to opt out of the problem than fail in it once more, and consequently a characteristic of this type of child is that he may lack the spirit of inquiry which typifies primary school children of higher abilities.

Mary, aged nine, was working with a mixed-ability group on a frieze. She was a non-reader and was being encouraged by another member of the group to help with sticking on some cut-outs. Her response was, 'I can't do it. I'll spoil it.' Children in this category need very special help to elicit the first tentative moves towards participation. Coleman (1966) in one of a series of articles on exceptional children points to the need to do this and links the approach with discovery learning when he reports: 'the creation of a favourable learning atmosphere and of a need to learn encouraged the reactivation of the child's normal tendencies towards exploration (reality testing) and self-development which had typically been discouraged by repeated failure in the school situation, or by insecurities and emotional difficulties in the home or by both.'

The most successful attempts to use discovery methods with slow learners which I have seen while mounting this inquiry have stemmed from an interest related to the day-to-day experiences of the children. Presentation of more unrelated themes has had less success. A teacher catering particularly well for slow learners related several instances where she had presented material which seemed to hold much promise. She observed the children's responses and saw that the learning was almost incidental to the set provision. It was only when she took the incidental interest and developed it that discovery learning was possible. Stephen, aged seven, had been working with capacity measures and water. After some aimless activity he suddenly turned some of the measures upside-down and began to drum on them with a paste brush. The rise and fall of the notes interested him and in great delight he informed the teacher, 'I made up a tune'. This initial interest was taken by the teacher and developed by the introduction of chime bars. Soon Stephen was busily recording his experiments and discovery with absorbed interest. Similarly, Derek, aged seven, had been set to work on a collage but was soon distracted and played with the newspaper, dipping it in the water. This rather negative approach was interrupted by the teacher.

'What's going to happen to that paper?'

'It'll melt.'

'Why do you think it will melt?'

'Cause it will.' (Typical finalistic response.)

Directed on to a more purposeful activity of seeing which commodities were soluble, Derek came across an assignment card. He asked the teacher to read it to him but was unable to continue as it was 4 p.m. He followed up the suggestion from the card at home. He had to find out if newspaper absorbed water more quickly if it was soapy. He told the teacher of preparing two jars, one with water and one with water and soap. 'I couldn't use that one because it was too thick.' (Obviously he had put a large amount of soap powder in the small jar.) He went on, 'I made it soapy by pretending to wash my hands in it in a bowl, then I poured it into the jar.' This was a very apt discovery about the quality of soap powder by this boy whose reading age is reported as five years. The discovery had purpose, meaning, and significance and again stemmed from a peripheral activity which was related to an everyday situation and the task on hand. Learning for learning's sake didn't appeal to Derek but this activity certainly did. This incident also illustrates the role of the teacher as initiator. One of the problems the inexperienced teacher finds is how to organize his time. A characteristic of the less adept teacher is that he rushes about, trying to do everything and be everywhere. In the first instance, the concentration of effort should be on the initiation of activities, especially with slow-learning children who do not readily find their own activities in the first place. Then a check should be made, but intervention may not be necessary if the activity is proceeding well. Every teacher must make the time to stand back and establish priorities of action. Many failures are the result of becoming totally immersed in a mass of activities, and failing to see where personal action can be most effective.

It has been shown in earlier chapters that the atmosphere of a discovery classroom should encourage discussion and the free and orderly exchange of ideas and views. This helps less able children. The give and take of thoughts, and the social milieu of group interaction, can help to clarify ideas and promote new ones which may lead on to more finding out. Two girls were looking out of the classroom during a snowstorm: 'It's snowing faster over there.' 'Yes but if you were over there—it would look faster here.' These two girls became very interested in the properties of snow, tested out their theory, and followed up what was, for them, a very relevant line of inquiry. There is a lesson for the teacher here. The problems raised by other children in the course of spontaneous conversation are often much nearer to the child's needs and more appropriate to his stage of development than many adult ideas which look good only to the teacher.

Students' observations of children in practical learning situations abound with instances of less able children learning by discovery. In PE, a group of such children were having difficulty in translating movements on the ground to movements on the large apparatus. It was only when the teacher took a specific movement and talked about it, analysing the parts and building them up into a composite whole that the children were able to develop the movement in a new situation. The relationships had been broken down and the sequence more readily seen. The final act of discovery, using the movement on the apparatus, was left to the children. This same situation often occurs in mathematics with slow learners. Indeed, mathematics has been described as 'a discovery of relationships and the expression of the relationship in symbolic (or abstract) form' (Schools Council, 1965). There is no virtue in calculating for its own sake. Slow learners should first of all be encouraged to think and try to understand the simplest of relationships and proceed, often by simple steps, structured by the teacher, to investigate tasks of greater complexity which are important to them. Then, computation may be used to aid understanding. This was illustrated by a mixed-ability group who had been out conducting a traffic census. The two leaders, both bright children, had devised a system of coding to chart different kinds of vehicles and vehicles seen more than once, etc. In fact the less able children had not fully understood this arrangement and the symbolic representation and had, therefore, taken little or no part in the charting of the information. However, on their return to school, they were very keen to help with the analysis of the data. The teacher extracted a part of the data involving only four categories of vehicles. She explained how one category was coded, helped the children to decipher the next group, and before she could withdraw gracefully, the others had 'cracked the code', and were determined to proceed with the subsequent charting unaided. Here the final insight into the problem was a discovery but the material had first been carefully selected and presented.

Much support can be found for the use of discovery

methods with less able children. Morris (1951) strongly supports this theme. He says 'Much indeed would be gained if, as teachers, we should come to place less reliance on drill, repetition, and the slow building-up of blind habits and devote the energies saved in this way ... to devising learning situations that would help the dull learner to gain insight into his problems and to learn, as the bright child does, by the active organisation of his own experience.' Morris is also greatly concerned about what can be done to improve the quality of the dull child's learning experiences. He concludes: *'In general, the answer is simple: let the learning situation be such that the learner can understand what he is doing and let repetition be used not to memorise meaningless associations but to consolidate by driving below the level of consciousness that which has first been understood by an act of immediate insight.'* This approach is really making a plea for teachers to present natural learning situations of direct interest to children and to arrange for children to investigate them until they can reformulate them easily in their own terms. These personal re-statements are the repetitions which will help slow learners to consolidate concepts already acquired.

The teacher has always to be aware of the solution which is appropriate only to one individual child. It may be novel, it probably will be unique, and it almost certainly will be unconventional. The case of Joseph is just such an instance. A very slow learner, Joseph was, at ten years, a non-reader and virtually a non-starter mathematically. However, the teachers all thought that he had some ability. School had become a drudgery to him and he suffered it. The class teacher and headmaster discussed the case and sent for the boy.

'You don't like mathematics, Joseph do you?'

'No Sir.'

'Right, you don't have to do it any more.'

A look of incredulous disbelief spread over Joseph's face. The headmaster explained that he could do exactly as he wanted. He asked if he could go to the farm. This, being his only known interest, had been anticipated and the visit arranged with the farmer. Each day Joseph reported at school and went off to the farm with instructions to report back later. He was engaged in conversation about his activities until eventually he was asked to find out various facts and statistics from the farm. How many eggs that day? How many of each grade? How much fodder given to the cattle? Could he think of any other information which would be useful?

He did and in fact he engaged wholeheartedly in a process of discovery which completely changed his attitude to school. This is a success story as Joseph's reading ability became almost average during the next six months. His mathematical ability also improved dramatically. This is an isolated incident but in this case, the procedure was followed and did work. The whole point of this anecdote is to pinpoint an individual solution which may be appropriate. This solution obviously was right for Joseph.

Massialas and Zevin (1967) conducted a wide ranging, fact-finding, exploratory investigation into discovery learning. Their work studies the approach with less able children. They find grounds to support a discovery approach with these children and say, 'The low I.Q. students (i.e., students whose I.Q. was in the 80-90 range) were capable of performing such intellectual tasks as defining the problem, hypothesizing, drawing logical inferences, gathering relevant data, and generalizing.' I have tried here to throw into relief some of the problems facing a teacher adopting discovery methods with slow learners, to illustrate that less able children can use the principles noted by Massialas and Zevin, and also to highlight some of the successes that have been noted by teachers using the method. It must be pointed out that the suggestions here have been found useful in working with slow learners but the approach is at variance with that encounted in discovery learning with brighter children. Both approaches have their place in discovery methods but it is important that the difference in the presentation for slow learners is emphasized.

9

Discussion topics—a miscellaneous selection of in-tray exercises, simulations, and instructional discourses

In this short chapter, a series of topics for discussion are presented. Sometimes, the topics are simple statements which may elicit discussion, but more often, they are presented in a way which it is hoped will encourage a more practical dialogue, drawing on real and imagined situations. The topics are wide-ranging and not all will be suitable for every reader, or group. The advice is to pick relevant topics and use them creatively to help to develop a dialogue which may assist to clarify some of the principles introduced earlier, and may also assist in solving individual classroom problems.

1   You have just taken over the headship of a school which has formerly been organized on traditional lines. You propose to make certain changes over the next twelve months. Itemize some general changes you would make in trying to implement a more informal ethos, and *either* construct a brief from which you could speak to a parents meeting to inform them of the changes you propose, *or* write a letter informing parents of these changes.

2 You are a class teacher and have been using discovery methods in a third-year, unstreamed junior class. A colleague working on more formal lines in the same school doubts the validity of your approach and wishes to discuss your different methods. Write down the main points of your argument in support of your use of discovery methods.

3 The diagrams show classroom plans. Discuss the relative values of each type of classroom plan as areas for

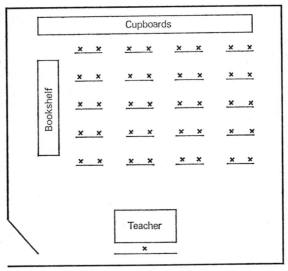

Figure 2: Classroom A

employing discovery methods where the accent is on individual and small group instruction.

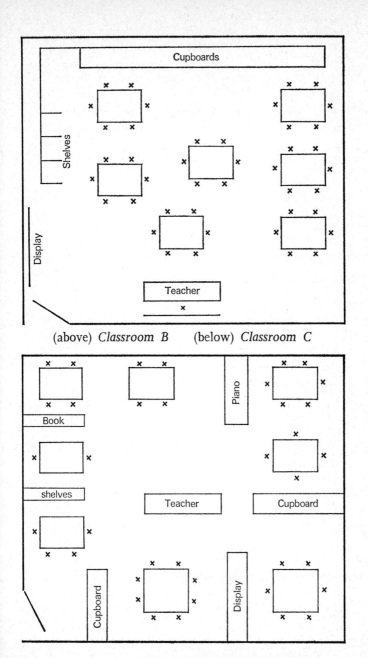

(above) *Classroom B*   (below) *Classroom C*

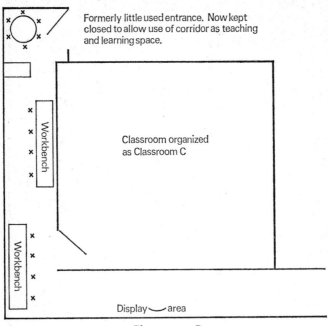

Formerly little used entrance. Now kept closed to allow use of corridor as teaching and learning space.

Workbench

Classroom organized as Classroom C

Workbench

Display area

Classroom D

4 If you were writing an architect's brief for a new junior school, what educational aims would you ask him to bear in mind (enumerate these briefly)? What practical ideas would need to be incorporated into the building for you to work towards the achievement of these aims? (Make a list of these practical features.)

5 Do discovery methods have equal value for all children? What are the implications for the teacher of (a) a positive, and (b) a negative answer to this question?

6 Are some subject areas more appropriate for discovery learning than others? Are there any practical implications here for the teacher?

7 'The rhythm of the day's work is varied between groups and individual activity.' By what criteria does a teacher decide how this rhythm shall be apportioned?

8 'Undoubtedly this method (inferential, informal, individual learning) works only by taking a very flexible view of what should be learnt.' Is this view a necessary concomitant of an informal approach to learning?

9 What is the teacher's role in a discovery learning situation? It seems that there are many strategies. Most teachers provide cues which lead to generalization through leading questions and prompts. They guide the discovery by providing gaps to be filled by the pupils. Sometimes, a sequence of learning is arranged by the teacher. Often children check their own reasoning, and the reasoning of others in the group.

Action: list a range of teacher-activities used in teaching by discovery approaches. What does the teacher do? Express this in clear, simple statements.

10 Is a discovery teaching technique more successful with a group than with an individual? Whatever your answer, what factors influenced you in making it? There is evidence on this point—see Shulman and Keislar, *Learning by Discovery* (Rand, McNally), page 131.

11 'Identifying a problem often helps to solve it.' Can you identify the main problems which a teacher may meet in changing over to a more informal style of teaching? State these simply, so that your list may be used as a guide to inexperienced teachers. Also indicate, just as briefly, how the problem may be tackled, or avoided.

12 The following letter was received by a head teacher who was attempting to use informal methods and discovery techniques in school.

Dear Head teacher,

I am disturbed about the education which my boys are receiving with you. Tony (aged 8) seems to spend most of his morning making models, drawing plans, playing with wooden blocks and doing something called Movement. His afternoon seems to be passed idly scanning books in the library, and, I suspect, copying large sections from them. James (aged 11) carries on in much the same way but also spends a great deal of time wandering about the village on a series of time-wasting ploys.

May I respectfully ask, sir, what sort of Education is this. Why are you not giving them a basic grounding in arithmetic and English which is the basis of their schooling. When are they going to get down to serious work. I admit they are happy but I am worried about the secondary school—I don't want them in the 'C' stream there.

Yours sincerely.

How would you answer these comments, allegations and charges?

13 Most of the situations posed here have concerned the 'birth pains' of adopting discovery approaches. What are the problems which may be faced by a school after several years of operating on informal, discovery lines?

14 'Worth pondering, too, is the fact that so many research studies report no significant differences in the results obtained from the adoption of some of the latest and most high-powered techniques of instruction. The biggest variable in the learning situation is the learner himself.' In this context, how does the teacher decide on the efficacy of methodological change?

10

A list of children's books useful for discovery learning approaches

This list indicates series of books, together with the publisher, which will be found useful in primary schools organized along active, discovery lines. Individual titles within the series will be found in the publishers' own catalogues which are readily available in schools and college libraries. The list cannot be exhaustive but is indicative of the material available to teachers.

E. J. Arnold: We Discover; Discovering Science; British Wool Kit; Vanguard Fully Validated Programmes; Let's Make Something; Dial for Discovery.

A. & C. Black: Looking at Geography; Looking at History; Looking at Nature; Let's read and find out series; Black's *Children's Encyclopaedia*; Black's Junior Reference Books.

Blackie: Know About books; All Around series; People at Work; Our Wonderful World.

Blackwell: How it Works series; Nature Books for Children; Pets' Series; Little Learning Library; Blackwell's Topic Packs; New Ways in Geography; The Discovery Books; Blackwell's Learning Library.

Blandford: Approaches to Environmental Studies series; Nature Study Class Reference series.

Bodley Head: Natural Science picture books; The Study books.

Brockhampton: Knight books; Picture Reference series.

Burke: Exploring Science; Let's Visit; Every Child's Book of ...; The Changing Scene; *The Junior Bible Encyclopedia*.

Cape: Jackdaw series.

Chambers: New Worlds to Conquer; People at Work; Starting Science.

Collins: Environmental Studies worksheets; Junior New View Histories; Science Project Experiments; Do You Know About?

Dent: Behind the Scenes.

Evans: Many Cargoes; Visual Geographies; History at Source; History, Topics and Models; Visual History books; Maths Adventure; Studying Nature; When You Think of ...; Let's Find Out; I Want to Know.

Hart-Davies: What Happens?; Expression; Environmental Studies (Schools Council Project Material); Observe and Learn; Mathematics Topics; Activity and Discovery in Mathematics; Life Then; Finding out about Geography; Finding out about Science.

Heinemann: Junior Science series; Science Workbooks; Focus books.

Hope & Sankey Hudson: *To Point the Way*; various Brightway series.

Hulton: Magpie books; The Exploring series; Essential Geography; Lively History; Round the World Histories; Global Activities; Read and Discover.

Longmans: Longmans Little Books; Discovery Programmes; All About ...; Town and Country; Live and Learn; Long-

mans Birds; They Work with Danger; Photographic Work
Cards; Environmental Workshop.

Macdonald Educational: Junior Reference Library;
Monarch books; Wonderful World series; Purnell Library
of Knowledge; Max Parrish colour books; They Lived
Like This; Famous Events.

Mills & Boon: Serving our Society.

Muller: The Modern World.

Oxford University Press: Clarendon Biographies; Lives of
Great Men and Women; *Oxford Junior Encyclopedia*;
Inside and Outside books; The Clue books; Living Abroad;
How They Were Built; The Modern World; Children's
Reference Library.

Penguin Education: Penguin Primary Projects Books.

Pergamon: The 'Theme-Scheme'.

George Philip: Unit books; Let's Wander books; Orbis
Pictures; Various atlases and wall-charts.

Schofield & Sims: Moving into Drama; Everyday Things;
The Young Investigator; Data; Panorama; Know Your
World; I Can Do It; Phoenix; In History.

University of London Press: Dolphin science books; Spot-
light on History; Discovery reference books; Finding Out
books.

Ward Lock Educational: Starter Kits; Information books.

Warne: Fun with Natural Science; The Observer pocket
reference books; Approaches to Primary Science series;
Children Around the Shores of the Mediterranean;
Various wall pictures; English Historic Costumes; Social
Studies Readers.

Wheaton: The 'Explore and Discover' cards; The Look
Around You series; The Read About It series; Animal
Studies.

Wills & Hepworth: Ladybird books.

Other publishers whose catalogues should be studied for relevant source material include Allen & Unwin, Batsford, Cassell, Chatto & Windus, Constable, Davis & Moughton, Dryad, Educational Productions, Galt, Ginn, Harrap, Holmes McDougall, Macmillan, Methuen, Murray, Nisbet, Oliver & Boyd, Pitman, and Routledge & Kegan Paul.

11

Some personal conclusions

One of the aims in all the schemes described in this book is the desire to improve the quality of learning, discernment, and attention. Mace (1962) shows one way towards achieving this through two features very common in primary school children when he says, 'The ultimate source of efficiency in observation, in memory and in constructive thought is insatiable curiosity and the will to know.' This reinforces a salient point made in chapter 1 regarding the nature of discovery and its relationship to learning. Throughout the book, this same curiosity and will to know has been a characteristic of many children whose behaviour I have described. These qualities are allies in the learning situation. My submission is that they are best used if children work from a point of interest and are allowed the facilities to branch out from this. The role of the teacher then is to guide, co-ordinate, and structure the ensuing learning situations in order to raise the children's standards, quality of approach, and level of thought. Often it is in the establishment of initial contact with a growth point or an idea that the teacher's special talent can be employed. It is when the enthusiasm of the teacher engages a child so that he wants to follow up the interest that one can point to successful teaching rapport. The skilful teacher is able, subsequently, to draw out the children's interests and sustain *their* adventure, enterprise, discovery, and achievement. The emphasis here is on 'their' because it needs real understanding and professional skill to do these things and still retain in the children the feeling that the growth and development is emanating from them. It is on the ability to lead out the children's initial interests into new, more fruitful areas that the teacher will be judged.

More and more in primary schools today the idea of what must be regarded as 'basic' is changing. Years ago we had the 3 Rs. Today, these Rs of reading, writing and arithmetic, still of fundamental importance, are taught as skills, the need for which emerges from children's involvement in the really basic work in what I have called the 3 Ms of Music, Movement and Manipulation. Through the 3 Ms, some children described in this book achieved the motivation which lead them on to a more purposeful study of the 3 Rs, the relevance of which could be seen when these were needed as tools to express the real interests at hand. Through their work in the 3 Ms, children are given the chance to look at themselves, their companions, teachers, and the world around them. It is through expression, taking roles, and in play that children are able to come to terms with human relationships and their environment, and the facilities for a happy, all-round development are provided. Commentators have noted that we have three selves: as we are, as we would like to be, and as other people see us. If the school can provide conditions where these three selves can grow to a wholeness where they are all recognizably the same, this would seem to be a further basis for sound development.

The recourse to books was certainly one of the chief common features in each of the schemes. Wherever the starting point, sooner or later it was necessary for children to turn to books for reference. Because of this, it is essential that books for the primary school should be chosen with care; books to suit a range of ability should be available on all major areas of work. There should be books to meet differing tastes, books to enlarge on possible topics, and suggest further areas for thought and possible new lines of development. Books should be profusely and skilfully illustrated and some books should be bought as a source of ideas from which children can develop their own lines of inquiry. Children should have a working knowledge of the library, be able to use the system of checking, find a book by using the catalogue system, and through use of and joy in books, come to love them and care for them. Books, then, being central to all the work carried on, must be presented so that the very display draws out from the children an urge to explore them. 'We must help the child to choose his books so that the ineffaceable impressions will be worth while', says Fisher (1961), but I would also add that a wide choice of books should be available so that a child is able to learn to assess and discriminate between them for himself—it is only through an early and constant experience of this kind of choosing and categorizing that the qualitative assessments necessary for the judgments of propaganda and mass media generally can be built up.

One sometimes wonders why many teachers who subscribe to most progressive educational thought do not, in fact, carry out these practices in their own classrooms. I believe that, in fact, most teachers are still hidebound by their own schooldays, early training and first appointment supervision. Too many still see a fund of knowledge which must be taught, essential facts to be learned and comparisons of usually inaccurate results to be made. Perhaps easing of selection requirements will alter these conditions. One thing seems certain, and this is that 'in-service' training courses must be widely extended to do two things; first, to give teachers an opportunity to reformulate their own philosophies of education and re-appraise their work in school, and second, to enable them to be put in touch with current trends, literature, experiments, aids, equipment, and ideas. Of these two aims, I would rate the first considerably higher than the second because unless the teacher really sees himself in true perspective and desires to look at change objectively and receptively, the second aim will be lost.

Another point which I rate of primary importance is that parents must be kept more fully aware of aims, ideals, and goals in schools. Too often, these have not been fully understood and efforts have been unwittingly undermined by parents not in possession of the full facts about the pattern of school life. The triangle of parent, teacher, and child must be durable yet flexible, firm yet malleable, understanding and understood. Meissner (1956) says 'All the time there is somebody who wants to push them [the children] in this direction or that, when there is a constant need for "the young to learn to breathe, to be quiet and to receive".' Only a sympathetic understanding of common problems by the teacher and parent can bring about the optimum conditions required for good growth and development of children.

Susan Isaacs (1930) repeatedly points out the need to

leave children to develop fully at each phase of development, whether this is seen as a step, stage, ramp, threshold,
or slope. As this book has, I hope, shown on numerous
occasions, the children themselves often know better than
we do what is right for them in particular circumstances.

All the work described in this book has been carried
out in physical conditions which were far from ideal. The
school buildings were conceived as an amalgam of classrooms, with one hall for assemblies, designed for children
receiving class instruction. Imaginative teachers have
slowly adapted these buildings so that they catered more
efficiently for the children in them, adventuring freely
without the shackles of 'the lesson' or 'their seat'. Doors
were taken off, inside partitions removed, work bays and
various corners devised for individual interests and group
involvement. It is interesting to note that in the experimental school buildings now being built many of these rather
makeshift ideas are being incorporated into architect-
designed, custom-built units. The accent is on open-plan
arrangements and split-level design with work corners for
a number of functions and free access to a variety of
learning situations. There is an emphasis on shared facilities, and the unit catered for specifically is not the class
but the individual child, learning by discovery methods.
The new buildings themselves pre-suppose new techniques.
Indeed it would be impossible to work under a rigid, formal
arrangement in the open-plan school. In this area, planners,
administrators, teachers, and children seem to have dove-
tailed their joint interests and enterprise to produce a base
which is truly a fitting unit for the widening of horizons
which characterizes primary education today. It is pipe
dreaming to pretend that all schools will be built with
these provisions in the near future, but inventive, creative

teachers will alter their own buildings to facilitate children's learning in the natural ways envisaged in this book.

New ideas must not be adopted because they are in vogue. They must be tried by a teacher as part of the practical application of empirical research findings. When innovation is in operation, a teacher must know exactly why he is taking a particular action; how he is going to organize the resources, both human and material; and what are the skills involved in acquiring the content to be learned.

I stop here by completing a paragraph from the National Froebel Foundation evidence to the Plowden Committee, quoted in part earlier, which I feel best sums up the spirit of this investigation and which points the way for our future work with children in school. Referring to the work of the primary school, the unity of learning and the value of creative work, they say, 'The activity we are thinking of is born out of curiosity and thrives wherever there is freedom for personal investigation and discovery. In this it is closely allied to the beginnings of scientific learning. For the child, the sense of delight and growing satisfaction in "creating"—whatever the medium—is more important than the actual end product.'

References

ASH, B. and RAPAPORT, B. (1960), *Skills in the Junior School*, Methuen.

AUSUBEL, D. P. (1963), *The Psychology of Meaningful Verbal Learning*, Grune.

BARKER, D. (1965), 'Primary school science', *Educational Research*, February, p. 155.

BARTLETT, F. C. (1954), *Remembering*, Cambridge University Press.

BARTLETT, F. C. (1958), *Thinking*, Allen & Unwin.

BASSETT, G. W. (1970), *Innovation in Primary Education*, John Wiley.

BEREITER, C. and ENGELMANN, S. (1966), *Teaching Disadvantaged Children in the Pre-school*, Prentice-Hall.

BLYTH, W. A. L. (1965), *English primary education*. Vol. 1: Schools, Routledge & Kegan Paul.

BRUNER, J. S. (1961), 'The act of discovery', *Harvard Educational Review*, No. 31, pp. 21-32.

CHALL, J. S. (1967), *Learning to read: The Great Debate*, McGraw-Hill.

COLEMAN, J. C. (1966), A series of articles in Magory, J. F. and Eichorn, J. R., *The Exceptional Child*, Holt, Reinhart & Winston.

REFERENCES

CUTFORTH, J. A. and BATTERSBY, S. H. (1962), *Children and Books*, Blackwell.

DEARDEN, R. F. (1968), *The Philosophy of Primary Education*, Routledge & Kegan Paul.

DONALDSON, M. (1963), *A Study of Children's Thinking*, Tavistock.

FISHER, M. (1961), *Intent Upon Reading*, Brockhampton Press.

FOSTER, J. (1971), *The Middle Years of Schooling: Recording Individual Progress*, Macmillan.

FOSTER, J. and SELBY, D. B. (1966), *To Point the Way*, Thos Hope & Sankey Hudson.

FREEMAN, J. (1969), *Team Teaching in Britain*, Ward Lock.

GARDNER, K. (1969), *Crisis in the Classroom*, Hamlyn.

HADOW REPORT (1931), *The Report of the Consultative Committee on The Primary School*, HMSO.

HOLLAMBY, L. (1962), *Young Children Living and Learning*, Longman.

HOLMES, G. (1952), *The Idiot Teacher*, Faber & Faber.

ISAACS, S. (1930), *Intellectual Growth in Young Children*, Routledge.

KERSCH, B. Y. and WITTROCK, M. C. (1967), 'Learning by discovery: an interpretation of recent research', in De Ceccho, J. P., *The Psychology of Language, Thought and Instruction*, Holt, Reinhart & Winston.

LURIA, A. R. (1961), *The Role of Speech in the Regulation of Normal and Abnormal Behaviour*, Pergamon.

MACE, C. A. (1962), *The Psychology of Study*, Penguin.

MARSH, L. G. (1968), *Let's Explore Mathematics* (Books 1-4 and Workbooks), Black.

MASSIALAS, B. G. and ZEVIN, J. (1967), *Creative Encounters in the Classroom*, Wiley.

MATHEMATICS DEPT, MANCHESTER COLLEGE OF EDUCATION

(1969), *Guidelines in School Mathematics* (chart and notes), Hart-Davis.

MAYS, J. B. (1962), *Education and the Urban Child*, Liverpool University Press.

MEISSNER, E. (1956), *A Boy and his Needs*, McDonald.

MORRIS, R. (1951), *The Quality of Learning*, Methuen.

MYCOCK, M. A. (1966), 'A comparison between children in horizontally grouped and vertically grouped infant schools', unpublished M.Ed. thesis, University of Manchester.

NATIONAL FROEBEL FOUNDATION (1965), 'Finding out Activities in the Primary School', *Froebel Journal*, No. 1.

PEDAN, C. (1964), 'A new pattern for the primary school', *Head Teacher's Review*, May.

PLOWDEN REPORT (1966), Vol. 1: *Children and their Primary Schools*, Central Advisory Council for Education.

REID, L. A. (1962), *Philosophy and Education*, Heinemann.

RIDGWAY, L. and LAWTON, I. (1965), *Family Grouping in the Infants' School*, Ward Lock.

ROWE, A. W. (1959), *The Education of the Average Child*, Harrap.

ROWELL, J. A., SIMON, J. and WISEMAN, R. (1969), 'Verbal reception, guided discovery, and the learning of schemata', *British Journal of Educational Psychology*, November, Vol. 39, Part 3, pp. 233-44.

RUSSELL, D. H. (1956), *Children's Thinking*, Ginn.

SCHOOLS COUNCIL (1965), *Mathematics in Primary Schools*, Curriculum Bulletin No. 1, HMSO.

SHAPLIN, J. T. and OLDS, H. F. (eds) (1964), *Team Teaching*, Harper & Row.

SHULMAN, L. S. and KEISLAR, E. R. (1966), *Learning by Discovery: a critical appraisal*, Rand, McNally.

SPENCER, H. (1963), *Essays on Education*, Dent.

REFERENCES

SPENS REPORT (1939), *The Report of the Consultative Committee on Secondary Education*, HMSO.

SPROTT, W. J. (1958), *Human Groups*, Pelican.

WARWICK, D. (1971), *Team Teaching*, University of London Press.

Bibliography

Please see the references to the form and use of this Bibliography on page 4. The books given in the References are excluded from this list.

ASH, B. and RAPAPORT, B., *Creative Work in the Junior School*, Methuen, 1957.

ASHTON-WARNER, S., *Teacher*, Secker & Warburg, 1963.

ATKINSON, M., *Junior School Community*, 2nd edn, Longman, 1962.

BARKER, C. *et al.*, *The 'New' Maths for Teachers and Parents of Primary School Children*, Arlington Books, 1965.

BAILEY, E., *Discovery Music with Young Children*, Methuen, 1961.

BILBROUGH, A. and JONES, P., *Physical Education in the Primary School*, University of London Press, 1963.

BLYTH, W. A. L., *English Primary Education*, Vol. 1 : *Schools*, Vol. 2 : *Background*, Routledge & Kegan Paul, 1965.

BOARD OF EDUCATION, *Handbook of Suggestions for Teachers*, HMSO, 1937.

BOYCE, E. R., *The First Year in School*, Nisbet, 1953.

BREARLEY, M. (ed.), *Studies in Education: First Years in School*, Evans, 1963.

BIBLIOGRAPHY

BREARLEY, M. (ed.), *Fundamentals in the First School*, Blackwell, 1969.

BREARLEY, M. and HITCHFIELD, E., *A Teacher's Guide to Reading Piaget*, Routledge & Kegan Paul, 1966.

BRITTAIN, J. (ed.), *Studies in Education: The Arts in Education*, Evans, 1963.

BROWN, M. and PRECIOUS, N., *The Integrated Day in the Primary School*, Ward Lock, 1968.

CATTY, N., *Learning and Teaching in the Junior School*, Methuen, 1952.

CENTRAL ADVISORY COUNCIL FOR EDUCATION (Plowden report), *Children and their Primary Schools*, Vol. 2: *Research and Surveys*, HMSO, 1967.

CHURCHILL, E. M., *Counting and Measuring: An Approach to Number Education in the Infant School*, Routledge & Kegan Paul, 1961.

CLEGG, A. B., *The Excitement of Writing*, Chatto & Windus, 1964.

COOPER, GERTRUDE E., *The Place of Play in an Infant and Junior School*, National Froebel Foundàtion, 1963.

CREBER, J. W. P., *Sense and Sensitivity: The Philosophy and Practice of English Teaching*, University of London Press, 1965.

DANIEL, M. V., *Activity in the Primary School*, Blackwell, 1949.

DAVIS, D. C., *Patterns of Primary Education*, Harper & Row, 1963.

DE LISSA, L., *Activity Methods for Children Under Eight*, Evans, 1964.

DIENES, Z. P., *Mathematics in the Primary School*, Macmillan, 1964.

DOTTRENS, R., *The Primary School Curriculum*, UNESCO, 1962.

DOUGLAS, J. W. B., *The Home and the School: A Study of Ability and Attainment in Primary Schools*, MacGibbon & Kee, 1964.

ENNS, F., *All My Children: A Year in a Junior School*, Hamish Hamilton, 1960.

FOSTER, J., *Creativity and the Teacher*, Macmillan, 1971.

GAGG, J. C., *Beginning the Three R's*, Evans, 1959.

GARDNER, D. E. M., *Education Under Eight*, Longman, 1949.

GARDNER, D. E. M., *Long Term Results of Infant School Methods*, Methuen, 1950.

GARDNER, D. E. M., *The Education of Young Children*, Methuen, 1956.

GARDNER, D. E. M., *Experiment and Tradition in Primary Schools*, Methuen, 1966.

GARDNER, D. E. M. and CASS, J. E., *The Role of the Teacher in the Infant and Nursery School*, Pergamon, 1965.

GATTENGO, C., *A Teacher's Introduction to the Cuisenaire Gattengo Method of Teaching Arithmetic*, Educational Explorers, 1962.

GODDARD, N. L., *Reading in the Modern Infants' School*, University of London Press, 1958.

GOLDMAN, J. M., *The School in our Village*, Batsford, 1957.

GOLDMAN, J. M., *Brave New School*, Hodder & Stoughton, 1965.

GOLDMAN, R., *Readiness for Religion: A Basis for Developmental Religious Education*, Routledge & Kegan Paul, 1965.

GOLDSWORTHY, G. M., *Part-time Nursery Education*, Nursery Schools Association, 1964.

GRAY, V. and PERCIVAL, R., *Music, Movement and Mime for Children*, Oxford University Press, 1962.

HOLT, J., *How Children Fail*, Pitman, 1967.

HOLT, J., *How Children Learn*, Pitman, 1968.

HUEY, J. F., *Teaching Primary Children*, Holt, Reinhart & Winston, 1965.

HUME, E. G., *Learning and Teaching in the Infant School*, Longman, 1948.

ISAACS, N., *The Growth of Understanding in the Young Child: A Brief Introduction to Piaget's Work*, Educational Supply Association, 1961.

ISAACS, N., *Piaget: Some Answers to Teachers' Questions*, National Froebel Foundation, 1965.

ISAACS, S., *The Children We Teach*, University of London Press, 1932.

ISAACS, S., *Social Development in Young Children*, Routledge & Kegan Paul, 1948.

JACKSON, B., *Streaming: An Educational System in Miniature*, Routledge & Kegan Paul, 1964.

KELLERMANN, M., *Two Experiments on Language: Teaching in Primary Schools in Leeds*, Nuffield Foundation, 1964.

KNELLER, G. F., *Introduction to the Philosophy of Education*, Wiley, 1964.

LANGDON, M., *Let the Children Write*, Longman, 1961.

MANN, B. F., *Learning Through Creative Work*, National Froebel Foundation, 1962.

MARSHALL, S., *An Experiment in Education*, Cambridge University Press, 1963.

MATTERSON, E. M., *Play with a Purpose for Under-sevens*, Penguin, 1965.

MELLOR, E., *Education through Experience in the Infant School Years*, Blackwell, 1950.

MINISTRY OF EDUCATION, *Primary Education: Suggestions for the Consideration of Teachers*, HMSO, 1952.

MINISTRY OF EDUCATION, *Primary Education*, HMSO, 1959.

MORRIS, J. M., *Reading in the Primary School*, Newnes, 1959.

NATIONAL FROEBEL FOUNDATION, *Children Learning through*

Scientific Interests, National Froebel Foundation, 1966.

NATIONAL UNION OF TEACHERS, *Nursery-Infant Education*, Evans, 1949.

NATIONAL UNION OF TEACHERS, *The Curriculum of the Junior School*, Schoolmaster Publishing Co., 1958.

NORTH-EASTERN JUNIOR SCHOOLS ASSOCIATION, *Basic Requirements of the Junior School*, 2nd edn., University of London Press, 1960.

NUNN, P., *Education: Its Data and First Principles*, Arnold, 1920.

NURSERY SCHOOL ASSOCIATION OF GREAT BRITAIN, *Planning the New Nursery School*, University of London Press, 1947.

O'CONNOR, D. J., *An Introduction to the Philosophy of Education*, Routledge & Kegan Paul, 1957.

PETERSON, A. D. C. (ed.), *Techniques of Teaching*, Vol. 1: *Primary Education*, Pergamon, 1965.

PHILIPS, H. and MCINNES, F. J. C., *Exploration in the Junior School*, University of London Press, 1950.

PICKARD, P. M., *Psychology of Developing Children*, Longman, 1970.

RAYMONT, T., *Seven to Eleven*, Longman, 1946.

READ, K. H., *The Nursery School: A Human Relationships Laboratory*, 3rd edn., Saunders, 1964.

RICHMOND, W. K., *The Teaching Revolution*, Methuen, 1967.

ROBERTSON, J., *Young Children in Hospital*, Tavistock, 1958.

ROSS, A. M., *The Education of Childhood: The Primary School Today—Its Growth and Work*, Harrap, 1960.

SCHOOLS COUNCIL, *French in the Primary School*, Working paper No. 8, HMSO, 1966.

SEALEY, L. G. W., *The Creative Use of Mathematics in the Junior School*, Blackwell, 1961.

BIBLIOGRAPHY

SEALEY, L. G. W. and GIBBON, V., *Communication and Learning in the Primary School*, Blackwell, 1962.

SIMON, B. (ed.), *Non-streaming in the Junior School: A Symposium*, PSW (Educational Publications), Leicester, 1964.

SIMPSON, D. and ALDERSON, D., *Creative Play in the Infants' School*, Pitman, 1952.

TAYLOR, C. W. (ed.), *Widening Horizons in Creativity*, Wiley, 1964.

TUDOR-HART, B., *Toys, Play and Discipline in Childhood*, Routledge & Kegan Paul, 1955.

TUSTIN, F., *A Group of Juniors*, Heinemann, 1951.

YATES, A. and PIDGEON, D. A., *Admission to Grammar Schools*: Report of NFER, Newnes, 1957.